Never the Same Again...

A young woman's story of life in the Blackstone Valley in the 1820s

by Phyllis Hosken Masso

Discovery Enterprises, Ltd.
Carlisle, Massachusetts 1998

All rights reserved. No part of this book may be reproduced, stored in a retrieval system, or transmitted in any form or by any means, electronic, mechanical, photocopied, recorded, or otherwise, without prior written permission of the authors or publisher, except for brief quotes and illustrations used for review purposes.

Copyright Phyllis Hosken Masso, Whitinsville, MA 1998

ISBN 1-57960-046-8

Library of Congress Catalog Card Number 98-71875

10 9 8 7 6 5 4 3 2 1

Printed in the United States of America

Subject Reference Guide:

Never the Same Again...
by Phyllis Hosken Masso

Industrial Revolution — YA Historical Fiction

Canals — Historical Fiction

19th Century Family Life — Historical Fiction

Dedication:

To the residents of towns in the Blackstone River Valley National Heritage Corridor in Massachusetts and Rhode Island, especially to the students and staff of the Whitinsville Christian School.

Credits:

Back cover illustration by Christi Masso Byerly.

Note: A glossary of terms, in alphabetical order, pages 145-147, explains the words highlighted with an asterisk in the text.

Table of Contents

Chapter 1
July 4, 1828 5

Chapter 2
The Walk to Uxbridge, August 1828 18

Chapter 3
William Works on the Canal, September 1828 26

Chapter 4
The Canal Opens, October 6, 1828 30

Chapter 5
The Funeral 35

Chapter 6
We Laugh Again, November 21, 1828 42

Chapter 7
Thanksgiving 1828 48

Chapter 8
A Cold Winter Begins, December 1828 53

Chapter 9
Lucretia's Birthday, January 18, 1829 59

Chapter 10
A Visit from Judge Whipple, Early in February 1829 62

Chapter 11
Our Declaration of Independence, Mid-February 1829 69

Chapter 12
Family Matters, March 1829 72

Chapter 13
A Letter for Sarah, Mid-March 1829 77

Chapter 14
Our Family Upset, April 1829 81

Chapter 15
My Twenty-first Birthday, May 1829 91

Chapter 16
A Visit from Cyrus, June 1829 97

Chapter 17
Independence Day, July 1829 106

Chapter 18
Cyrus and Betsey, End of July 1829 113

Chapter 19
Another Letter from William, End of August 1829 119

Chapter 20
Cyrus and I Make Plans, September 1829 125

Chapter 21
Our Plans Change 128

Chapter 22
A Letter from Cyrus 140

Postscript from the Author 142
Glossary 145
About the Author 148
Acknowledgments 149

Chapter 1

July 4, 1828

    The sound of muskets firing jolted me from my sleep, and I heard the faint sound of bells in the Northbridge Congregational meeting house, two miles away, ringing wildly. Panic came over me until I was awake enough to remember it was Independence Day*, and I, Betsey Carpenter, was safe at home in Sutton, Massachusetts, with my mother and nine younger brothers and sisters. I wanted to roll over and go back to sleep, but the bells and musket shots served as an alarm for Miranda, who eagerly woke up Mariah and Abigail, who shared her bed. They ran down the stairs to the kitchen and began banging on pots and pans to begin the celebration.

    Thank you, Lord, that Independence Day comes but once a year. I rubbed my eyes and groaned a greeting to Sarah and Nancy who had been asleep beside me in the garret*.

    Nancy pulled the night cap off her long reddish blond hair and sighed, "Oh no, now they woke up the baby and Lucretia, and they're crying. Poor mother. All that banging right next to her room."

    "I'll go calm Lucretia down," I told Nancy. "Mother will have her hands full with the baby." *Lord, it's going to be an effort to act cheery. I'd rather be asleep. I hate to wake up this way. Why do they need to make so much noise? I need your help.*

"Remember," Nancy said, "we used to do the same thing on Independence Day at their age. I'll see if I can quiet them down a bit. While I'm up, I might as well get the milking over with. I'll get William to help me." We both knew from experience it was useless to try to get Sarah to help. On the rare occasion that she did help, she was such a daydreamer that she took twice as long. Even then, the cows weren't fully stripped of their milk.

William was splashing cold water on his face from the pump outside. "Where's Jonathan?" he called out. "He's probably making the racket in Northbridge Center."

This was the first year that Jonathan had participated in the May militia* training so now he was allowed to be in the Independence Day celebrations. Last year, no one from our family was in militia because Father had died of consumption* the year before and Jonathan was not eighteen yet.

"Why didn't he ask me to go along?" he grumbled. "I helped him clean the musket."

"I know," I said, joining him outside. "I saw you two taking the whole thing apart and pouring boiling water down the gun barrel. I'm sure it hasn't been cleaned that well in years. I hope it still works."

"It works all right," he said. "Didn't you hear us fire it? I hope it doesn't misfire today or just get a flash in the pan*."

"I saw you measuring gunpowder into those little paper pouches like father used to do. What's to keep you from shooting someone accidentally?"

"Girls don't know anything. We didn't use musket balls, just the gun powder. All we want to do is make noise." He kicked the ground angrily. "Why do we hafta be eighteen to join the militia? I can hunt."

"Don't let Mother hear you say that. She thinks eighteen is too young," I said. "Hey, William, how about helping Nancy with the milking?" I asked.

"That's woman's work. When you gonna teach Mariah and Abigail to milk? They're as old as you were when you learned," he said. He, too, knew it would be useless to teach Sarah, though she was nearly as old as he was.

"We'll teach them soon, but we need your help today."

"Oh, all right. But don't make a habit of it. My hands are numb from gripping that scythe all day."

"I hope Jonathan can stay home from the mill a few more days to help you with the mowing," I said.

He shuffled off toward the barn, rubbing his hands together, mumbling to himself.

I listened for the sound of the brook flowing in from Burt's pond, past our grist mill and dropping off to flow under the dirt road and off into the woods. It always soothed my spirits.

Nancy managed to get Miranda, Abigail and Mariah to stop banging on the pans in the kitchen. "You girls get washed up while William and I go milk. Then we'll have some Indian pudding for breakfast," she said, starting the fire in the kitchen fireplace and filling the kettle with water. "In fact, get dressed and go pick the last of the strawberries to put on top of the pudding," she called out.

The sun was just coming up and a few beams of light came in through the windows. A faint breeze caused the curtains to flutter. The rooster began to crow. I went into Mother's room off the kitchen and picked up five-year-old Lucretia, sobbing in the bed. I wiped her nose, rubbed her back gently and pushed her honey-colored hair away from her face.

"Good morning, Mother. Lucretia, did all that noise scare you?"

"Ya," she answered, sniffing and gulping loudly, burying her head against my neck.

"It frightened me at first, too. I think that's Jonathan firing his musket with some other boys," I said, giving Mother a knowing glance. "Remember, today is Independence Day, and all the people are happy and celebrating. We're going to town for games and a big picnic with lots of people. Remember when we did that last year?"

Lucretia sniffed and swallowed hard and nodded her head. I hugged her and put her down on the floor. "You go quickly to the necessary* and then wash up in the kitchen. I'll ask Abigail to comb your hair and braid it with pretty ribbons. I think you're big enough to wear the red dress that used to be Miranda's if I just quickly take up the hem a bit. You can play Hen Coop and Chicken with your friends." I wiped her eyes and then gave her a gentle push to send her on her way.

Mother said, "I hope Jonathan will be careful with the musket. It seems that every Independence Day someone gets hurt with the muskets, the cannon, or those 'crackers.'"

"Don't worry about Jonathan, Mother. He may be fun-loving, but he knows how much we count on him," I assured her.

Mother slowly took off Harriet's wet clout*, hung it up to dry, pinned on a dry one, and began nursing her. Harriet calmed down and grabbed onto a strand of hair that had fallen out of Mother's nightcap. She sighed contentedly as she twisted Mother's long dark hair around her tiny wrist and energetically nursed.

Mother had become fretful since Father and two-year-old Silence died within a month of each other. Father's lingering fight with consumption had drained her strength and her spirits. His constant coughing and heavy breathing was hard for all of us to bear. Mother no longer sang while doing her housework, and getting through the work every day was such an effort.

We scurried around the house, washing up, getting breakfast, and making a picnic lunch of sliced cold meats and cheese, fresh bread and a variety of pickles. Then, we put on our prettiest summer dresses and new bonnets. We girls had been getting ready for this event for days. Nancy packed the strawberry tarts we had been making over the last few days to sell.

Jonathan ran into the house, devoured some breakfast and changed into the militia "uniform" that he had created. He strapped the leather box containing the gunpowder packets to his waist and punched William playfully on the shoulder.

"The musket fired just fine. Thanks for your help," Jon said.

"Ya coulda woke me up and let me come along," William said sourly, punching him back a little too hard.

"You gotta grow up, first, Will," he said, wrestling a little with him. Jon was tall, lean and strong and looked so handsome in his uniform. Will was muscular from months of planting, and mowing and soon had Jon pinned to the floor. "Sorry," Jon gasped. "I take that back. Next time, I'll take you along." Will let him go.

Little Lu ran up to Jon and exclaimed, "You scared me when you fired your musket, Jonafun," wrinkling her brow and fixing her little mouth into a pout.

"How could I scare a big five-year-old girl like you, Lucretia?" he said, tugging on her braids. "You're going to hear even louder noises than that. We're going to fire the cannon up by the meeting house today after the big procession. Be sure to cover your ears. You'd better hurry up so you can see me march with the militia. You'll hear a nice big drum and two people playing their fifes, and we will all march like this." He grabbed her hand and began an exaggerated march around the table, whistling "Yankee Doodle" and slapping his free hand on his knee to imitate a drum. In no time, her pout was gone and she was giggling.

"Betsey is humming Miwanda's wed dwess for me to wear, Jonafan. Do you fink I'll be pwetty?" Lucretia asked.

"*Hemming*, not humming. I'm sure the whole town of Northbridge will notice what a pretty little girl you are," he said, tickling her in the side. "I gotta go meet at Deacon Bachelor's," he said, running out the door, making a point to avoid Mother, who looked ready to scold him.

I ran for the door to keep it from banging and saw him racing to catch up with the men on French Road who were making their way to Northbridge Center.

Soon, we all were ready to leave. William carried the basket with our dinner, mumbling about having to go with a bunch of women. I carried the pies and Nancy had the tarts. Mother carried Harriet, and Sarah carried an empty jug, which she would fill with water near the meeting house, adding the powdered citron packet to make lemonade.

"Did you remember your shoes, Sarah?" I asked.

"No," she said sheepishly and ran back to the house for them. I waited for her, grateful for the chance to hear the brook again. I sat on the high stone wall which formed the dam for our grist mill and looked back at our house, with its steep roof and big center chimney. A mockingbird in a tree beside the house recited its list of bird songs, one minute sounding like a songbird and the next like a chickadee. I would have liked to sit there much longer just enjoying the peace and quiet, but Sarah soon came out carrying her shoes, and we caught up with the others.

"Miranda, you hang onto Lu's hand, and keep her to the side of the road," Mother said.

Miranda grabbed Lucretia's hand and immediately began reciting "Peter Piper picked a peck of pickled peppers," never missing an opportunity to educate her younger sister. When Lucretia was with Miranda, she tried harder to act grown up.

The inseparable Abigail and Mariah brought their game of The Graces along, which Uncle Benjamin, Father's brother, had made for them. William told them it should have been called The Clumsies, since more often than not the girls missed catching the hoops with the sticks and then had to clumsily run after them and pick them up, their long dresses often making them trip.

As we passed the Goldthwaite farm, we joined other townspeople. All the children were barefooted, and dry dirt curled up between their toes. Grasshoppers jumped and flew out of their way as they raced to cool their feet in the spring at the top of the hill. "Don't get your dresses wet," Mother called out. The children turned back, nodded, waved, and were soon out of sight on the winding, hilly road.

It was a glorious day, and everywhere we looked the fields were full of corn, nearly knee-high now. It wouldn't be long before it would grow so high you wouldn't be able to see the neatly laid stone walls, bordering the fields. A few maples and oaks lined the farm road providing some relief from the blazing sun.

Constantine Goldthwaite came out from her house and called out, "Hello, Betsey. Mrs. Carpenter, may I carry Harriet?"

"Certainly. She is a wiggly one, though, I will warn you. I'm nearly breathless carrying her up this hill," she said, handing Harriet to her.

"Oh, you're a heavy one all right. Yes, you are. You have grown so much since I saw you last. Look at all those teeth. Ow. Don't bite me! Is she a year yet?" Constantine asked.

"Yes, she had her first birthday in April."

Our conversation quickly turned to which young men might be there today.

Mother interrupted, "I was married and had a child (Betsey, in fact), at your age. Actually, I was married at seventeen, Nancy's age."

I glanced at Nancy in her beautiful blue dress and bonnet. Her bonnet was tied loosely on and pushed back as is considered fashionable. Her reddish blond hair shone in the sun.

I said, "I am in no hurry to be married, Mother. Besides, I doubt that any young man will pay any heed to just plain Betsey when she has a sister as pretty as Nancy nearby."

"Betsey, don't be silly. I am not interested in marriage at my age," Nancy said. Then lowering her voice to imitate a man, she said to me, "And you look simply ravishing."

We all laughed, baby Harriet included. As soon as we reached the meeting house, Abigail, Mariah and Miranda spotted friends and ran to play with them. Sarah was content to walk around by herself.

We took our picnic basket and jug of water to the tables that had been set up and then watched the procession. Lucretia clapped her hands in delight seeing Jonathan march in his uniform to the beat of the drum, and she marched in place. Her excitement was contagious and Mother and I smiled at each other. I had forgotten how pretty Mother could look. It seemed so long since she had smiled. Her lavender dress and matching bonnet made her look younger and healthier today. No one would be able to tell that her own hair was starting to turn gray with the dark artificial curls attached at the side of her bonnet. Mrs. Bishop had helped her attach the curls, which were made from some of my hair that we had saved when I had had several inches cut off when I was twelve. *Lord, thank you that Mother is happy today.*

The militia continued their procession up to the meeting house where they fired their muskets a few times and then prepared to fire the cannon. The sergeant shouted the orders. "Ten vent... Search piece... Sponge piece... Handle cartridge... Load cartridge... Ram cartridge... Prime cartridge... Make ready... Fire."

We covered our ears, but no matter how prepared we were for it, the cannon firing still made me scream and Lu cry. Harriet jumped even though Mother had held her head close and covered her ears. Mother looked to see if any of the men had been hurt, especially Jonathan, and breathed a sigh of relief. We had made it through a Fourth of July firing without an injury.

It was announced that the Independence Day speech would begin in about fifteen minutes. Nancy took the opportunity to mingle in the crowd selling tarts. Nobody really wanted to hear the annual speech so they took their time ambling to the meeting house, each one murmuring that they hoped it wouldn't last too long.

Dr. Crane, the minister from the Northbridge Congregational Church, was walking toward Mother and me, gesturing for us to wait. He was several inches shorter than either of us, but his top hat made it not so obvious. At first we assumed he was coming to speak to someone else and looked behind us. He had his usual wad of chewing tobacco in his cheek, and turned and spat the dark brown juice on the ground. My stomach turned. I remember Father saying he would do that even when he was preaching. Father had attended Northbridge Congregational as a young man and said many of the men spat tobacco juice during meeting. The floor was quite slippery by the end of the service. I was glad our South Sutton Second Baptist church didn't allow tobacco.

He tipped his hat politely and adjusted his spectacles. "Widow Carpenter and Betsey, how are you, and little...I'm sorry, I can never remember the names of all your little ones," Dr. Crane said. "As the Psalmist said, 'As arrows are in the hand of a mighty man; so are children of the youth. Happy is the man that hath his quiver full of them.' Your quiver is certainly full. How many children are there again? I've lost track of your family since I moved over here to the county road."

Mother answered, "There are ten, but I can hardly call some of them children any more. Betsey here is twenty and Jonathan eighteen. At that age, I was a married woman with a family."

"Mother, I am very happily unmarried at twenty and glad not to be a young mother," I replied.

Lu tugged at my dress and motioned that she wanted to tell me something. I bent down and listened as she eagerly whispered in my ear, "Tell him the baby is Haywiet, and I'm Lucwetia, and I'm five and a half," she said.

"Rev. Dr. Crane, Lucretia wants you to know that the baby is Harriet, she is Lucretia and she is five and a half," I said.

"Of course, my dear Lucretia. I am so glad to make your acquaintance. You look as if you might be ready to start school soon," he said.

"My sister, Miwanda, taught me my ABCs. I can spell my name. L-U-C-R-E-T-I-A," she said proudly.

"Well, I see you can," he said as he winked at me. "And Widow Carpenter, it is about school that I wanted to talk to you bwiefly, I mean briefly if I may." He chuckled. "When I was observing the Union School at the end of winter term, I noticed how bright your daughter Nancy was. I talked to the schoolmaster about her, and he said she was one of the brightest students he had." He began looking above Mother's head, and finally even closed his eyes as he continued talking. "We have a need in Northbridge next winter term for a teacher and, with your permission, I would like to talk to Nancy about that. As I understand, she is seventeen years old, is she not?" His eyes fluttered open, and he turned and spat upon the ground again.

Mother and I couldn't help wincing and looking at one another as Rev. Crane took out his handkerchief and wiped a little of the brown juice trickling out of the side of this mouth.

"Yes, she will be seventeen in two weeks. Rev. Crane, I'm sure she would be very pleased to have you ask her, but she is so young to teach winter term when all the older boys would be attending, don't you think?" Mother asked.

"Normally, we wouldn't ask young women to teach winter term for that reason, but I watched your Nancy. She is very mature, and with two brothers in the house, she has had experience in dealing with young men," he replied. "By the way, I noticed your Jonathan shooting with the militia today. What a remarkable likeness to his father, Samuel. It doesn't seem that long ago that Samuel was that age and he and his brother and widowed mother came to town. They bought the property where you live now and began attending the Congregational meeting house here where I am the minister. I hated to see him go when he married you and joined the Baptists in South Sutton, but I certainly understand."

Rev. Crane looked off at the sky, seemingly lost in memories for awhile, then added, "Do come visit us sometime. Your husband did not sell his pew* before he passed on, so it is still there for you—up in the gallery, I believe. My, time goes so quickly. You have another son besides Jonathan, don't you?"

"Yes, William, over by the tree," she answered.

"And how old is your William now?"

Lucretia yelled out, "Jonafun was fiwing Father's musket, Rev. Cwane, and Willy is fourteen."

"Yes, Lucretia, your father would be proud of him. Fourteen, eh?" Rev. Crane looked at William leaning against a tree across the meeting house yard all alone. "I'm surprised William isn't joining in a game of rounders.*"

"He took his father's death very hard, Dr. Crane. He hasn't been the same since. Samuel had been teaching him how to make ploughs. When he took ill, William couldn't seem to bring himself to work alone, and he hasn't touched the tools or ploughs since. He is so melancholy. He is a big help with chores around the house and farm, but seldom talks unless he is spoken to."

"That is such a shame. There's many a farmer in Northbridge, Uxbridge, and Sutton using Samuel's sturdy wooden ploughs. I myself used them every year. In fact, I just replaced them this year with ones I saw at the county fair last fall, made by a Mr. Howard in Hingham. They have a cast iron plough-share that should last longer than the wooden ploughs and are much easier to use. They just glide through the earth. Even a child could plough with them, which is what I need, being so short you know," he said with a chuckle.

"I don't know how you find time to do all you do, farming all that land, writing sermons, and preparing young men for college," Mother said.

"Some of my best sermons come to me while I'm farming. I just stop what I'm doing and jot the idea down, and then continue ploughing or mowing. I've taught the young men I train to do the same. They help with the farming. Working with God's creation is good for us all. To get back to the subject at hand, with your permission, Widow Carpenter, I would like to talk to Nancy quickly before the speech. Are you willing to grant it?" he asked.

Mother hesitated a moment and shifted little Harriet to her other hip. "I suppose there would be no harm in mentioning it," she said, while poking some stray hair back into her bonnet and adjusting the artificial curls.

"Thank you, ma'am. Good day to you and Betsey and L-U-C-R-E-T-I-A and Harriet," he said as he shook little Harriet's hand. Harriet pulled her hand away. Tipping his hat, he left us and walked briskly toward Nancy, and turning to the side, he spat out the disgusting brown tobacco juice again.

Mother said, "I didn't want to be contentious and besides he didn't give me time to speak, but your father did not become a Baptist because of me. His grand-father had been a Baptist minister years ago in Norton, and your father started attending the Baptist meeting house before we knew each other. In fact, that is where we became acquainted." She reached up and adjusted her bonnet and the dark artificial curls as if setting the bonnet on straight would set the record straight as well.

The meeting house bells soon began to ring, and everyone assembled for the speech. We didn't want to sit up in our pew in the gallery; it would have been too hot, and the children would not have wanted to sit still anyway. We stayed outside but moved over by an open window. The members of the singing school sang a selection, and I was happy to hear Mother hum along.

Colonel Bachelor began the usual Independence Day speech. "Just two years ago we celebrated our fiftieth year as the United States of America."

Several men yelled out, "Hear, Hear."

"Our town has grown considerably since 1776 when we had a population of less than 500. Now, it is nearly a thousand. Many of you have grandparents or great-grandparents who fought for our freedom," he continued. Mother turned to me and smiled knowingly since we all had been told that father's grandfather, William Carpenter, had fought in the American Revolution. "Some gave their lives and others their fortunes. My grandfather, for one, was said to have mortgaged his farm to pay his soldiers. I challenge you to covet that costly freedom and work to keep our nation strong. One way this can be done is to vote this year in the election..."

I turned to Mother and whispered. "No one in our family can vote this year. Jonathan isn't old enough. It is a shame that women cannot vote when there is no head of household. Who do you think you would vote for, Mother, if you could—John Quincy Adams or Andrew Jackson?"

She whispered back, "I'm partial to President Adams since he is from Massachusetts and has relatives here in town, but it troubles me that both candidates travel on the Sabbath. President Adams even campaigned on the Sabbath." She shifted Harriet to the other hip and continued. "And, I have heard that Jackson is not a very polished leader. He wants to have the government run by the common people. I don't know if most common people know how to run a government properly."

I added, "I know I should not listen to rumors, but I heard Jackson wasn't properly married and even killed at least one person in a duel over the matter."

"I don't know about that. I am just glad I don't have to vote."

Someone standing behind us motioned us to be quiet. Mother was embarrassed and didn't say another word. Actually, I was surprised that she had thought so much about it.

Col. Bachelor continued speaking, "Though many towns have people unemployed, God has blessed our town with new industry. We started out as a farm village with a couple of foundries and have become a highly successful mill town. The Whitin cotton spinning mill is growing rapidly with two thousand five hundred spindles now," he said as he turned and smiled at Deacon Paul Whitin and his sons. "And so are the many small shoe businesses starting up, the cooperage, &c*. I dare say, God's blessing may well be in response to the firm stand our town has taken on temperance*."

Several men yelled out in agreement, "Hear, Hear." Rev. Crane shook his head in disagreement. Everyone knew he did not agree with the Temperance Movement and in fact was heard to offer ardent spirits* to his hired help. He even owned the only cider mill in town. I would have thought a minister of the Gospel wouldn't behave in such a way. Mr. Whitin had tried to convince him of the merits of Temperance, but he wouldn't hear of it.

Col. Bachelor continued, "As you know, the new Blackstone Canal has opened in Rhode Island and hopes to be open all the way to Worcester by October in time for the cattle show, God helping us. Ladies, more pantaloons are needed for the Irish workers, and I ask that some of you may consider making some of them to take for sale at the store in the Rawson Tavern in Uxbridge. This simple patriotic act will benefit our state—our whole country, in fact, and bring you some added income."

"I hear those Irishmen are loud, mean rummies and papists besides," I whispered to Mother.

"Betsey, shame on you," she whispered back. "You know it isn't fair to judge people and pass on gossip. You don't even know any of them. Making pantaloons sounds like a good way for you to bring in some extra money. With your sewing skills, you could have some made up in no time. Even papists need clothes, you know."

Once again, the people behind said, "Shh."

I thought of myself making pantaloons for loud, mean rummies and Nancy teaching, and my eyes began to water a bit. I didn't want to teach, but it did sound more adventuresome than sitting at home sewing for Irish papists. I blinked away the tears and wiped my nose with my handkerchief. *I'm sorry, Lord. I'm feeling very jealous. Help me to be more content.*

Col. Bachelor finished his speech, and then gave recognition to the old men in the audience who had fought in the Revolution: Nathaniel Adams, Capt. Aaron Adams, and Col. James Fletcher. We all yelled, "Hip, hip Hurray" three times and then sang "The Defense of Fort McHenry,*" accompanied by a nice looking young man on his violin. An older woman loudly screeched out the high notes of "the laaaand of the free." "Yankee Doodle" with the fifes and drum, was then sung; it sounded much better. All the ladies hurried out to set their food on tables, each one seeming to outdo the others with choice meats and delicious pies and cakes. The militia men went across the street to the tavern to enjoy their meal together, and Jonathan stopped by to greet us.

"You scared me again when you fired the musket, Jon," Lu said.

"Was it just too loud for the prettiest little girl in Northbridge?" he asked, pulling on her braids. "I like that red dress on you. Can you play Hen Coop in it?" Lucretia quickly spun around, stopped, bent her knees slightly until the hem of her dress lightly touched the ground, making the skirt look like a big puffy tent.

She laughed and smiled at him. "I see you can," he said. "Well, I need to go join the militia men for dinner in the tavern. See you in a little while." He ran to catch up with the others. I only wished William had half his enjoyment of life.

Abigail, Mariah and Miranda stopped playing The Graces with their friends and came running over at the sight of food. Miranda complained, "Everyone throws the hoop too high and too far for me. They know I'm littler." A glance at the delicious food quickly put an end to that complaint.

Mother said, "Miranda, go find Sarah. She is probably somewhere reading a book or something. Her mind never seems to be where her body is."

Mother seemed to lose track of which children she had accounted for, so I added, "Abigail and Mariah, go tell Nancy to come join us." It was an effort for Mother to keep track of where everyone was and who was in charge of whom. One Sabbath day, we left for home without Sarah and were half-way home before we noticed. Sarah had not even realized we had left her when Jonathan went back for her.

"Miwanda, I told Rev. Cwane how to spell my name and he finks I'm weady for school," Lucretia said.

"You are so smart, Lucretia. Did you tell him I taught you?" Eight year-old Miranda had always played the role of teacher, as soon as she got home from school every day. "Come with me to get Sarah," she said.

As Nancy came over, several young men's eyes followed in admiration. She didn't seem to notice, but came up saying excitedly, "We're rich! I think I've sold more than two dollars worth of tarts! I can hardly wait until people stop using the French and Spanish coins. It will take me awhile to figure out exactly how much, but I know I did very well. And Mother, what do you think of Rev. Crane's asking me to teach? He told me he talked to you about it."

"I suppose I am not surprised that he should ask since I know you have always done well in school, but I find it hard to think of you moving away from home and..." She stopped and sniffed, blinking hard.

Nancy put her arm around her. "Mother, don't start crying. I'll just be a few miles away and I could come home on Sabbath. Please Mother. I'll be fine."

"You will be fine, I know. I wasn't expecting you to leave home before Betsey." She sniffed and attempted to smile. "I'm being so silly. It will have to happen sometime; it's just that I wasn't expecting it so soon. After all, I got married at your age. Of course, you can do it if you want to. I know you will be good at whatever you do." She gave Nancy a hug.

I got that old feeling back of being a failure to Mother. Well, it wasn't my fault that a suitable young man had not presented himself yet. *Lord, help me to live a life pleasing to you and be content waiting to be married if that is your will.*

Lucretia said, "Nancy, I want you teach at Union School. Den you could be teacher for me, Miwanda, Abigail, Mawiah and Sawah."

We lived in a section of South Sutton that was almost completely surrounded by the town of Northbridge, and the two towns shared the school. That is why it was called Union School. It was a nice, new, red brick one-room schoolhouse just a half-mile down the road from us.

"You can't teach where you want. Dr. Crane asked me to teach at another District School because the position is open. You already have a schoolmaster at Union School, and I am sure you will like him very much, Lucretia," Nancy answered. She turned to Mother and me. "Dr. Crane is going to introduce me to another new teacher named Rebecca Bradford. She is from Providence, Rhode Island, and has been teaching one year. He said she would have some good suggestions since she was so new herself. He has observed her and says she does a fine job. I hope he will be able to say the same for me. He observes the teachers in every school in Northbridge two times a year."

William had joined us by now and added, "He gets paid plenty for it, too. They pay him fifty cents per school just to observe."

"He is one of the most educated people in town, and I'm sure the town gets its money's worth from him," Mother said. "Over the years, in his home, he has prepared about one hundred young men for college, so I'm sure he knows what to look for."

"That may be true, but one of them told me he hardly feeds them anything when they are boarding with him. The miser," William said.

"William, I fear you're being slanderous. Please watch your tongue," Mother said. "Let's just drop this conversation and eat."

We enjoyed our picnic with several other families in the shade of a big maple tree along the road, and then I began to sell tarts in Nancy's place. I didn't sell nearly as many.

Independence Day was over with all too soon and our conversation on the way home was filled with plans for Nancy to teach and for me to sew pantaloons for the Irish.

Chapter 2

The Walk to Uxbridge
August 1828

    Jonathan bought several yards of denim for me at the company store across the street from where he worked at Paul Whitin & Sons in South Northbridge, and I dutifully sewed pantaloons for the Irish canal workers. I hoped they weren't loud and drunk. I reasoned that even if they were, they were still doing a great service for all the towns along the Blackstone River by building the canal. It is so exciting to think about canal boats bringing goods upstream clear from the ports in Providence, Rhode Island, and going north all the way to the center of Massachusetts. It is unbelievable to think of Worcester, Massachusetts, becoming a port city when it is nowhere near the ocean.

    William came in quietly from outside, wiping his brow and holding his hand out behind him to make sure the door wouldn't slam. He slowly crossed the room, his shoulders drooping, looking down at the floor as he walked past Mother, who was busy breaking up the curds of cheese into a cloth-lined basket and swishing the flies away. He sat in a chair across the room from me.

    "I finished mowing the rye this morning and tied it in sheaves along the fence. Betsey, you got any switchel* made? I'm parched," William muttered.

"I sure do. Miranda, go get some switchel from the root cellar. I didn't put in as much vinegar this time and I added a bit more molasses. I think you'll find it refreshing."

He wiped his sweaty forehead with his neck scarf and collapsed into a chair, breathing deeply with his mouth hung open and his eyes shut.

"William, we have both worked hard this morning. I finished the pantaloons, and since you finished the rye, why not take a break. Let's walk to Uxbridge to deliver these pantaloons. It's a little cooler today, and I think it would be good for us to get away. Maybe we can get a look at that canal, too," I said, hoping to catch his interest.

He kept his head tilted down but raised his eyes up and actually looked at me with a little interest. I was happy to see I had struck a positive note for once. He asked, "Are you sure you feel up to walking? It's five miles each way."

"Well, I must admit I would rather take a horse and surrey, but since we don't have either one, and it's reasonably cool, a long walk won't be too bad. I would like to get a look at these Irish that are going to be wearing my pantaloons and see how that canal is coming, too."

"Give me time to catch my breath and rest a bit," he said, taking the switchel from Miranda, drinking the whole glass without taking a breath and gesturing with his hand for more.

"Does anyone else want to come?" I asked. "Nancy, how about you?"

"It does tempt me, Betsey, but it feels so cool inside and I need to work on these dresses for teaching. Now that you are done with the pantaloons, I hope you will help me. You're a much better seamstress."

"You flatter me. Of course I will help. I love the cotton prints you chose. I fear the young men will have a difficult time thinking about their studies," I teased.

Mother sighed. "You two go ahead and go to Uxbridge and have fun. Nancy and I will stay at home and slave away."

"Now you make me feel guilty, Mother," I said. "I can stay and help if you want."

"No, I was teasing. You have hardly been out of the house since Independence Day. I am pleased with how diligently you have worked on those pantaloons. You deserve a break. I hope they fetch a good price. You need to cover the cost of the denim and profit about twenty cents on top of that, I think."

"We'll tell you all about the canal when we return," I said.

"When it opens up to Worcester, I plan to get over that way and watch a canal boat or two go by, but I must say, watching the construction doesn't interest me, nor does walking ten miles," she said. "You should pack a nooning and plenty of water. Have a good time. William, please just take the bucket of whey* to the pigs on your way out."

William poured the whey in the pigs' trough while I changed my dress and gathered up some slices of dried meat and cheese, a loaf of bread and a jug of lemonade. I combed my hair and put on a nice bonnet. William couldn't be persuaded to dress up a little for the occasion, not even to change his neck scarf. He put on his usual tall straw hat, and we quit the house. He insisted on carrying everything in a pack on his back.

"What a gentleman you are," I said. "What would I ever do without you?"

William looked straight ahead, but gave me a glance to the side, and I think I detected a slight smile. I wondered what we would talk about while walking five miles, since he had hardly spoken more than a sentence at a time since Father's death.

It turned out that I needn't have worried about that. It seems that walking, with just the two of us, in the out-of-doors on a cool day was just what he needed to open up what he had kept bottled inside himself for nearly two years.

"Betsey, being in the house and yard reminds me too much of Father's death. I've been thinking of leaving…of, of…moving somewhere."

"William, you mustn't talk that way. Remind yourself of Father's life and the things you used to do together when you see something of his lying around. As you hold the plough handle, remind yourself of how he held it and how he taught you to put all the pieces together. You can remember his life by carrying on his work."

"I wish it were that easy." He wiped his eyes with his sleeve and continued, "All I know is I just can't make myself pick up the plough handles. Last year, I just let the hay and rye reseed itself. I can't do that again this year; the roots will get all bound up. I just can't do it."

"Oh, William. I feel so bad for you."

He kicked a rock down the road for awhile, folded his arms resolutely in front of him, and set his mouth firmly shut…then finally began to speak again.

"When I hear of folks moving west to Ohio and Michigan territory or the new states of Indiana or Illinois, or going out to sea on a merchant ship or whaling boat, or moving to Maine, I get so excited. When I think of staying at our house, I just get depressed."

"This all takes me by surprise," I said. "Why do you think you have to move so far away? Why don't you build a little house on some of the property you inherited when Father died? Jonathan could keep living in our house, and you could build a new one. Or you could sell it and buy some other land in Sutton or

Douglas or Uxbridge or get a job in Worcester or Millville and come home every few months."

"You don't understand," he said.

I stopped walking, and looked right at him. "William, people die at sea, or never come back when they move out West or up to Maine. Oh, please don't talk that way. You have family here. What about Mother? She would be heart-broken to have one of her two sons move away." *Lord, help me be wise. I don't know the best way to talk to William.*

"It's hard to explain, Betsey. I don't know why I had to go bringing it up." He stooped to retie his shoe and adjust the pack on his back. We started walking again. "I don't have any plans made, and I'm not old enough to head out on my own."

"You're no child, William. In fact, you do a man's share of the work around the house and farm. Since Father died and Jonathan went to work in the mill, we depend on you. I have to remind myself that you are only fourteen. Who would plant and harvest the crops, bring in the wood and water and do the other hundreds of things you do each day?"

"I don't know. You'd survive, Betsey. There's so many of you girls; you could split up the jobs so nobody would have too much to do. Sarah, Abigail and Mariah are old enough to be helping more than they do. Even Miranda."

"Your work is man's work. We're not strong enough to plough fields and harvest," I said.

In my anxiety, I found myself walking faster. I had been hoping I could get William to talk to me; now I was wishing he hadn't said anything. I decided not to tell anyone about our conversation. There was no sense worrying anyone else.

We passed the Samuel Taft Tavern, so I took the opportunity to change the subject. "Father told me once that President Washington stayed there in 1789 when he was touring New England to see if they approved of his presidency," I told William.

"It couldn't have been 1789 if Washington was the first president. We got our independence in 1776," William argued.

"We didn't have a president right away, William. Didn't you learn your history lessons?" I scolded. "We were governed by a Continental Congress at first."

"Oh, I forgot," he said. "Well, that was a very long way for him to come from Washington, D.C."

"I think you have forgotten quite a lot. New York was the capital back at that time," I reminded him. "Our nation has changed so much since then. What exciting times we live in. I wonder who will be the next president."

William kicked a stone out of the road and said, "I don't care about such things."

He continued to think and plan aloud about a move out West, and in no time, we were in Uxbridge at the store in the Rawson Tavern where the pantaloons were to be sold. I showed William the initial "B" that I had cleverly worked into the stitching on the back of each of them. I thought it would be great fun if I should ever meet an Irishman in the future who was wearing a pair of the pantaloons I had sewn, though I doubted I would be bold enough to say anything about it. I was proud of my work and felt a part of this new enterprise that was sure to change each of the towns along the Blackstone River and canal.

I left the pantaloons at the store and was given forty cents credit for each pair; that covered the twenty cents of denim and gave me twenty cents in profit, just as Mother had hoped. *Thank you, Lord.* I wished I could have been paid in cash, though. I decided to make a purchase at a later time after the canal was open, when maybe the store would carry a nice shawl from China or something else I had never even heard of. I wondered if there was something I could get for Mother that would make her smile.

Uxbridge is such a busy place, and will be much busier when the canal opens because it's the half-way point between the Atlantic Ocean at Providence, Rhode Island, and the end of the canal in Worcester, Massachusetts. The canal boats will dock in Uxbridge overnight, bringing a lot of business to the inns and local farms.

The canal amazed me. We looked at it from the new bridge on the Post Road going near Mr. Capron's farm. It had no water in it yet and was so shallow and narrow. I had pictured something much bigger. It was only about six or eight feet deep and had sides that sloped in at the bottom. It was backbreaking work hauling all that dirt out. About a quarter of a mile down the canal, they were building a farm bridge across the canal where it had cut off access to part of Mr. Capron's farm land. Last fall and spring had been rainy and almost all the work on the canal had been destroyed. In His providence, God gave us a relatively dry summer. I was glad for the workers' sakes that today it was cool. I loved these August days that gave us a taste of fall but still had the green look of summer.

Some of the workers were using pick axes to dig while others were cutting trees or using oxen to pull trees up by the root. Oxen and horses, too, were being used to drag out heavy loads. Some of the men were using a funny triangular shaped cart they called a wheelbarrow. William and I had to laugh out loud; it looked so peculiar.

A young Irish workman turned around to see what was so funny, and the foreman shouted at him. "Fill your wheelbarrow and quit gawkin'." The Irishman wiped his forehead with his sleeve and muttered something under his breath. I felt bad that we had caused that to happen and wished I could tell him so. I couldn't help thinking that I might feel like cursing if someone screamed at me like that. *I'm sorry I caused that, Lord. Please bless that Irishman.*

The foreman measured the top of the canal opening and yelled again, "You've got to make it two feet wider here; it's only 32 feet."

"William, where do these men live?" I asked, feeling sympathy for them.

"I heard they set up camps along the construction sites, and live in canvas tents or in some places have dirty shanty towns," he answered.

"You mean after a hard day of work out in the sun, they have no real home to go to? What an awful way to live." I pictured them going to a lean-to of some kind and flopping down on a bed of hay. Suddenly our simple home seemed like a palace. *Father, thank you for our home.*

The foreman bellowing again at a worker who had stopped to rub his sore back caught my attention. "There's plenty more men wantin' your job if you're going to quit workin'. Fill your wheelbarrow or fill your jacket and move out of here." The worker winced and gasped as he bent over and forced himself to keep working, obviously in pain.

My stomach was turning, and I felt sick just watching. I wanted to shout at the foreman but was afraid it would get the Irishman in worse trouble. I didn't know what to do. That worker was probably my age; others were old enough to be my father. I pictured Jonathan, William, or Father working like that. Our family worked hard, but at least we weren't being yelled at.

William called out to me, "Come on. Let's walk over along the base of Goat Hill and have a look at one of those locks. Just keep out of the way of any workers."

That interested me and gave me a good reason to leave. The scene had magnetized me, and I was horrified at watching, yet unable to walk away. We walked slowly in silence to the lock, staying along the wide banking on the opposite side of the canal from the hill, to keep out of the way of men who were quarrying the granite on Goat Hill. The noise of their hammering the iron drills into the stone was jarring. My head began to ache. What a lot of work to break apart a rock! When they finally got a piece finished, the oxen dragged it down to be used for the walls of the lock. Casks labeled Dexter Lime were strewn about, their white powdery contents spilled around them. The masons were mixing up some kind of mortar with it.

"Do you know why the banking we're walking on has to be so wide and flat?" William asked.

"No, but I suppose you do," I teased.

"Because horses have to walk on it beside the boat, to pull it along," William said.

William gazed at the workings of the lock, fascinated. "I could never understand how they worked. I'm glad we had this chance to see them with no water in them. Look how the carpenter is hanging the doors; they will be in a V-formation when they are closed." he said.

A big, burly blacksmith was there, too, checking to see that the hinges he had made were working properly.

"It looks like a dungeon with those stone walls and doors at each end. It's so narrow compared with the rest of the canal. How would a boat even fit? It can't be more than ten feet wide. And so deep. It must be about fifteen feet deep. It would feel so eerie to go in with very little water, have the doors close and then feel yourself rising as the water filled it up. I hope I get to ride on a canal boat some day," I said.

"Oh, yes, the lady of leisure will ride to Worcester for the day, stay at an inn and return the next day. Maybe you should attend a ball while you're there," William teased. "Where would you ever get the extra fifty cents to pay for it?"

"Maybe I'll make more pantaloons and save my money, mister." Though I don't normally enjoy being teased, it was so good to see William in a playful mood. *Dear God, please help him stay like this when we get back home.* I was afraid to tell him how happy I was to see him like this again; he might become self-conscious and become melancholy again.

"You didn't answer my question. How do the boats fit?" I asked again.

"They're only about nine feet wide."

"How can they be so thin?"

"What do you mean, how can they be so thin? They're just built that way. They are only used in a shallow canal. They aren't big merchant ships with masts and sails for the ocean or those new steam-powered river boats, you know. They are more like a barge. They just float along a canal, being towed slowly by horses walking beside them on the tow path."

"I thought they used mules," I answered back, hoping to know something that he didn't.

"Have you seen any mules around here? They use mules on the Erie Canal that just opened in New York because the Dutch settled New York and they're used to them. We're going to use horses because our ancestors are English and that's what we use," he said. "By the way, did you know this Blackstone Canal is already open in Rhode Island? They've been making trips from Providence to a place called Scott's Pond since Independence Day."

We walked over to the river nearby, where it was much quieter, and enjoyed a picnic. We watched in silence as the tiny water spiders shot across the top of the water, stopping suddenly, then shooting off again. Little turtles climbed off rocks and plopped down into the water and swam away. A muskrat swam along at the water's edge, and William said he ought to bring his musket next time. There was a reward being offered for those who would hunt them, because they destroy the banks of the canal.

Suddenly, something that had looked like a dead piece of tree branch sticking out of the water, began moving. We looked over in time to see a blue heron lift its huge body into the air, jut its neck out with a funny crook in it, beat its mighty wings, and noiselessly soar above the nearby pines. Its wingspan was about four feet, and it took our breath away to watch it. "The Lord has such a sense of humor. That big bird is so ugly and beautiful at the same time. God must have had fun creating him," I said.

We walked home, and no more mention was made of William moving away. I hoped that he had had a good enough time to make him forget the notion. With nothing to carry, our trip home went quickly.

We arrived home in time to do the afternoon milking. Nancy and I milked while William fed, watered and combed the oxen. We could hear him mumbling something to them as he curried them. I heard the word "ploughing" mentioned a few times. He loved the oxen and called them his boys. He patted them firmly, and as he left the barn, we noticed him wiping his eyes with his sleeve. Sarah was in the barnyard and noticed him. She came over and put her arm around his waist. We could hear their conversation as we finished milking.

Sarah asked, "What's the matter, William?"

"Nothing. It's just that I know I'll have to plough soon, and I can't bear to handle Father's ploughs." He wiped his eyes and nose with his sleeve and adjusted his straw hat.

Sarah surprised us by answering, "I'll help you. I'll walk beside the oxen like you used to when Father ploughed and you were much younger. The oxen like me. I often go in the barn and talk to them when no one is around. I tell them how much I miss Father."

William nodded and cleared his throat, swallowing hard.

Sarah continued, "Remember how I used to hand him his tools when he and the other men were making ploughs in the shed? I just feel lost without him." She wiped her eyes as well, and they briefly hugged and went into the house.

Father, help me to be more considerate of Sarah and William.

Chapter 3

William Works on the Canal
September 1828

William walked to Uxbridge again, alone this time, carrying Father's musket. The building of the canal fascinated him and he especially liked watching the Irish use those new fangled wheelbarrows.

When he returned home, he said, "By next month, the canal should open. Betsey, guess what I saw. The same young Irish worker who got in trouble for looking up at us last month, and his pantaloons had a 'B' design in the cloth around the waist."

"You must be teasing." It made me laugh. Somehow it seemed I had helped him by sewing some new pantaloons, and I felt a little relieved.

"They need more workers to finish in time for the Cattle Show in Worcester," he said. "They're getting slowed down by all the locks they're needing to build in Millbury." He hesitated, shuffled his feet on the floor, and coughed. "Mother, I want to help them. Do you think all the girls could manage without me for a month or so if I split lots of wood ahead of time and carry a few of buckets of water in before I go in the morning?"

Mother looked up, encouraged to see him so excited. "I suppose so, William, except that on wash day, I can't imagine the girls being able to keep up with all the water that needs to be hauled."

"We'll manage, I'm sure," Nancy said. "We will just not fill the buckets as full, and we'll make more trips to the well. It's still nice enough to do the laundry outdoors anyway. We just need a few gallons in the house for washing dishes. I think you should let him, Mother."

"What about the ploughing?" Mother asked. "Who will do the ploughing?"

The silence filled the room. I just looked at my hands, Nancy fidgeted, and Sarah looked as if she could cry.

Jonathan seemed to realize how important it was for William to get out of the house. "I'll tell Mr. Whitin at the cotton mill that I need to take a few days off to help with ploughing," he said. "Mr. Whitin is used to that. A lot of the workers have land and need time off now and then during planting and harvesting."

"I'll help Jonathan," Sarah added.

Mother's mouth opened and she looked at Sarah astonished.

"I don't mean I'll plough; I'll lead the oxen along like William did when he was younger. I often go visit them in the barn, Mother. They're used to me, and I have always wanted to help with ploughing," Sarah said.

"Well, all right. And, Jonathan, are you sure Mr. Whitin will give you time off?" Then she hesitated. "We will lose the income from your work at the mill, though, Jonathan."

"I'll give you the income I get from the canal job," William answered. "They make more money than you do at the mill, and I just want to do something different."

He seemed determined, and Mother finally gave her permission. William began work the next day. He came home totally exhausted and filthy each evening. It seemed useless to wash up thoroughly only to get so dirty the next day, so he would just wash his face, neck and hands outdoors at the pump and then sleep out in the barn in the hay. I would have felt sorry for him except that he seemed so content. After two days of walking five miles each way, he decided to stay down with the Irish workers in their camp. He came home Saturday afternoon so he could attend Sabbath meeting with us the next day, though. We soaked his clothes is soapy water, boiled them and scrubbed them, knowing that by Monday night, our efforts would seem in vain.

One day he announced, "Betsey, I worked today with the young Irishman we saw last month. His name is Cyrus Delaney. He thinks you're pretty; you remind him of Irish girls."

I felt my face get hot. "Well, he obviously didn't look at me for very long that day, so he might well change his mind if he looked a little longer."

"I told him your name, and he said it over and over and smiled. 'Betsey. Betsey.' He likes the pantaloons you made for him, too."

"I didn't really make them for him, but I am glad he likes them." I found myself reddening even more and was anxious to change the subject. I don't remember any young man saying I was pretty before. And how could he like the name of Betsey? Just plain Betsey. Of course, if he saw Nancy, I'm sure he would find her prettier.

The next day at Sabbath meeting, Rev. Boomer solemnly climbed the winding stairs up to his pulpit and preached a fiery sermon warning of strange new religions, particularly of those claiming to receive new revelations from God. He reported that a young man by the name of Joseph Smith in Palmary, New York, had claimed to have found some mysterious tablets with writing in a foreign language. He said an angel told him the interpretation. We looked at each other in disbelief and Nancy and I stifled a laugh. Surely no one would believe such a thing. Rev. Boomer reminded us that God was not giving any new revelation to mankind and that all we needed was found in God's Holy Word, the Bible. Churches or individuals, or even angels were not to add to it. He also warned us of the Roman Catholic doctrines that might come creeping in since we had the Irish Catholic canal workers around; the 'papists'* gave their church and the Pope the authority that only God's Holy Word should have. I could not imagine how an Irish Catholic could influence any of us when we never interacted with them and were certainly not sitting down having theological discussions with them. My mind wandered to Cyrus Delaney and I looked at William. Why did an Irish Catholic have to be the one to think I was pretty?

The morning service ended and Mother said she was very tired and would never make it through the afternoon service, so we ate our nooning in the meeting house pew as usual and then William and I walked home with her. He and I took turns carrying Harriet and supporting Mother by her arm. Jonathan stayed with the others for the afternoon services. I wish we didn't live so far from the meeting house. A forty-five minute walk is too much when you're not feeling well, and it took us even longer because Mother walked so slowly. I don't remember this ever happening before. I was worried, but she said just sleeping was all she needed.

In the coming weeks, she seemed to do a lot of sleeping and had very little energy, so the rest of us made the cheese, baked the bread, did the laundry and tried to let her rest. Nancy and I decided this was as good of a time as any to teach Abigail and Miranda to do the milking. They learned it rather well but did not have much strength in their hands at first. After about ten minutes, they complained that their hands hurt and began shaking them around and rubbing them. That upset the cows, who began kicking, so Nancy and I finished up. I'm sure, in time, they will do fine.

Though Mother stayed in bed most of the time, she lay there fretting about all that needed to be done. "Remember to take three bushels of apples to Aunt Elizabeth and Uncle Benjamin. Have you washed the bed linens this week? Make sure the neighbors haven't left the waterwheel going at the grist mill. Did you pull up the last of the beans from the garden? Are you making cheese every day? Are we out of bread? You better boil Harriet's clouts. She is starting to get a rash. Did you bank the fire before going to bed?" And of course, lying in bed, she noticed how dirty the walls were, how smudged the windows, all the dirt on the floor, the dust on the furniture, the pictures not hanging straight on the wall, and on and on. She would have made a good sergeant in the militia.

Chapter 4

The Canal Opens
October 6, 1828

Mother insisted she was feeling better so we all walked the six or seven miles to the center of Uxbridge to watch the opening of the Blackstone Canal to Worcester. It was a beautiful fall day. The maples along the roads and stone walls were turning brilliant oranges and reds.

"Imagine what this must have looked like when the Indians lived here, and before all the trees were cleared for farming. The whole countryside would have been ablaze with color," I said.

The festivities were near the Capron Mill on the road to Mendon, farther than where William and I had walked a couple of months ago. Uxbridge has the looks of a city now with the the public house, the big Congregational church, Uxbridge Academy, the stores, a lumber yard and even the Blackstone Bank.

The canal had been in use since July in Rhode Island, but this was the first day it would be open all the way from Providence to Worcester. William was especially excited since he had helped to dig the canal. It was disappointing to him, of course, that they were unable to finish it in time for the Cattle Show in Worcester yesterday. Actually, there still was a little more to do on it, but it was close enough to being finished to open for use today.

A long, thin white barge named the *Lady Carrington*, bedecked with red curtains, floated by with about fifty people on deck, including several dignitaries waving and a band playing. Someone sitting on the back railing of the boat nearly fell in when one of the horses pulling the boat suddenly lurched forward at one point. All the bystanders laughed heartily.

Mariah was upset, though. "He could have drowned if he fell in."

"The water is only about three feet deep, so he would have just got a good soaking," I said, happy to contribute some knowledge about the canal.

"But why did the horse jump like that anyway?" she asked.

"Maybe he got stung by a bee or a horsefly," I answered. "It's a good thing that young man walking beside him had a good hold on him and calmed him down right away."

William added, "It's also a good thing the boat was going so slowly. The horses are only allowed to walk about four miles an hour."

Mariah was so concerned about everything. "Do those poor horses have to pull the boat all the way from Providence to Worcester?"

"No, they change horses about every fifteen miles. There are stables along the way for them," William informed us. "Any more questions?"

"Yes," Abigail said. "Why do they call the boat the *Lady Carrington*?"

William said, "They often name boats after women, and a man named Mr. Edward Carrington invested a lot of money in the canal so he named the boat after his wife. Most of the boats will be for goods, but this boat is mainly for passengers. They call it a 'packet.'"

This was such an exciting day. There were a number of important men from Northbridge and Uxbridge there. I saw Mr. Sylvanus Holbrook sitting on his white horse and looking so stately. He invested a lot of money in the canal, too. He has two mill villages in Northbridge named after him, Upper Holbrook and Lower Holbrook. Some of the fine broadcloth for William's and Jonathan's Sabbath shirts was made on the new power looms in his mills. All the Tafts and Whitins were watching as well. I wondered if all these mill owners had closed down their mills for the occasion. I found myself looking around to see if I could see any Irish workmen, and William noticed.

"The Irish aren't welcome in town unless they are working." William said sarcastically, "They are just loud, rummies, you know,"

I was sorry I had felt the same way at one time, too. I'm sure they were a rough lot, but now I was more inclined to understand why.

I looked over at Mother, and she was pale. "Are you all right, Mother?" Here, let me take Harriet. You sit down and have a drink of water."

"Is it hot out, or does it just seem that way to me?" she asked, seating herself carefully on a rock.

It wasn't very warm out and I became alarmed when I felt her forehead. "Mother, I think we better get you home. You have a fever. William, see if you can find someone with an oxcart. She's in no condition to walk seven miles home."

Nancy came over when she saw me bending over Mother and in no time at all had found Judge Welcome Whipple, our neighbor, and asked if Mother could ride home with him in his surrey. I would never have been bold enough to ask for a ride with a gentleman even though he was our neighbor and a member of our church. He was happy to oblige, though, and said he was ready to go right away since *Lady Carrington* was now out of sight. Nancy assured us that she would see that the rest of the family got home. *Thank you, Lord, for doing more than what I asked or thought.*

I rode along, propping up Mother somewhat and holding baby Harriet on my lap. Riding in the surrey was not much faster than walking, because the road was so rough, and the ruts in the road caused us to bounce around the whole way, but at least Mother didn't need to exert herself. Mother leaned her head against my shoulder and every once in awhile sighed deeply. Harriet somehow fell asleep through it all. At one point, Jonathan went running past us barefoot and was home before we were.

When we arrived home, Jonathan took Harriet and put her in her crib, and I helped Mother to her bed. I brought her cool cloths and gave her a drink of water. Judge Whipple offered to get Dr. Robinson, but Mother mumbled that she would be fine soon.

We expected Mother to improve quickly; she was seldom sick in the past and had always managed to get up to do her housework even when she didn't feel well. This time, however, her condition worsened. We prayed for her night and day. After a couple of weeks, Jonathan finally went to get Dr. Robinson on the county road on the hill near Northbridge Center, and he came on his horse.

"I have some herbal medicines that should help considerably," he said after examining her. "I wish you had called on me sooner, however, as your mother's fever is quite severe. Everything works best when an illness first begins. The fever shows that her body is trying to fight off a disease, but since she has had it so long without help, her body is weak and the cure, if it works at all, will take longer."

"Mother is never sick, and we just assumed she would get better," I replied. I wished he hadn't said, "if it works at all." What could he mean by that? *Lord, please help Mother get better.*

"Well, you did what you thought best. Now, I'll do my best to find out what is making her so ill. All illness can be traced to obstructed perspiration, but various things can cause this: sorrow of mind, too severe labor, sudden change of habit, wounds, unwholesome diet, &c. Can you think of anything that may have brought it on?"

I thought back over the last couple of weeks and could come up with only one thing. "The only thing that you mentioned is 'sorrow of mind.' Mother just mentioned recently that it was this time of year two years ago that Father and Silence died." I said.

Dr. Robinson replied. "Our state of our mind can diminish the active energy of nature and our bodies can become ill. Any kind of fever is caused from the body being cold. We will make efforts to warm your mother. Put some water on to boil, and we will bring her near the steam so she can breathe it in. I will mix up some medicine that will likewise raise her body temperature. See how she is shivering and shaking even now."

He began mixing some peppermint and water and then gave her a spoonful. I put a blanket around the kettle of hot water to direct the steam towards her face. Nancy propped her up. She was so weak, and hardly aware of us being there. Lucretia, Miranda, Mariah and Abigail all watched in silence.

"You children go out and play. There is nothing you can do for your mother, and I'm sure she will relax more with a smaller audience. Go on now," Dr. Robinson said.

They went out and began making piles out of the fallen maple leaves, but they clearly did not feel like jumping in the piles or hiding in them as they usually would have.

I looked out the window and saw Sarah sitting on a rock, staring off into space. The oak trees had turned gold, bronze and copper colored. How could it be such a beautiful day when Mother was so sick? William was combing the oxen briskly but looked preoccupied. I was glad little Harriet was sleeping. When Mother had become ill, it had been necessary to wean Harriet, but she was doing very well drinking from a cup, and only when she was overtired would she cry for Mother and pull at the front of Mother's dress.

After about an hour, Dr. Robinson left. He instructed us to repeat the medicine and steam several times per day and said he would come back tomorrow. He repeated that he only hoped he had not been called too late. I felt terrible. I was the oldest, and I should have sent Jonathan to get him sooner.

When Jonathan came home that night, he had a package tucked under his arm. After going over to kiss Mother and greet her, he reminded us that it was Mariah's tenth birthday and handed her the package which he had purchased at the company store. It was beautiful golden-colored yarn for her to knit herself new mittens and a scarf for winter. In our distress over Mother, we had lost track of days and all, even Mariah, had forgotten her birthday but him.

"I think you are old enough to start knitting something besides garters,* don't you?" he said.

She pressed the yarn to her face and began dancing around the room ecstatically. Jonathan had such a way of getting the girls to try new things. If I had told her she had to learn to knit mittens, it would have been a different story altogether.

For the next ten days, Nancy, Aunt Elizabeth, and I took turns caring for Mother day and night. We saw no signs of improvement. She slept most of the time and when she was awake, she could hardly speak at all. She would look at us with glassy eyes and just mutter single words. We fed her bread and weak soups and teas. It took two of us to help her to the chamber pot because she was so weak, though she seldom had to use it; the fever seemed to burn off all the liquids she consumed.

Every morning and evening, we gathered around her bed and prayed that God would heal our mother, just as we had prayed for Father and Silence.

Chapter 5

The Funeral

    Mother passed on today. I can't believe it's true. I had done my best to keep her warm and feed her clear broths, give her the peppermint medicine and steam, but it didn't help. Dr. Robinson came again at one point but couldn't offer any help. He repeated that he was sorry we hadn't called him sooner. It's my fault. I just thought mother would get better. I never dreamed God would take our mother, too, only two years after Father and little Silence.

    Our neighbor, Salmon Burden, offered to ride around to the various towns where relatives lived to tell them of her passing. There are so few neighbors with horses, we were glad to have him do it.

    Five-year-old Lucretia tugged at my apron and cried, "Who will be our movver now, Betsey?"

    I had just been asking myself the same thing. Surely no one would want to take in ten orphaned children. I wondered if the Selectmen would ask several families to take us in until we could be auctioned* in the Spring with the other poor people in town. I could not say such a thing to little Lu, standing there looking up to me with those trusting blue eyes, her hair pulling out of her honey-colored braids, and her face smudged from tears streaming down her freckled face. To her, I may have looked like a likely candidate for a mother. When you're five, a twenty-year-old sister seems so grown up. I remembered Mother's comment that at my age, she was married with a family. I may be old enough to be married, but not to have nine children. Though, as Mother often said, several of us were hardly children any more.

I picked Lucretia up and held her tight. My chin quivered, and I struggled to speak. My throat felt so tight and sore from trying not to cry. "I don't know who will be our mother, Lucretia. I don't know. Something will work out. God will take care of us." I sat down and rocked back and forth with her wondering what could possibly work out, and suddenly I couldn't hold back my tears any longer. What would we do? Lucretia pulled away and looked up at me, concerned, as I sobbed.

I felt so alone even though there were ten of us in the house. Aunt Elizabeth, father's sister, came over and washed Mother's body. How could I call Mother "a body?" Nancy made some attempts to help by bringing fresh water and towels.

"Let's put on her favorite lavender calico dress," Aunt Elizabeth said, awkwardly putting the dress on Mother's lifeless form. I couldn't watch and Nancy was unable to make herself help any more either.

It was the dress she had worn on Independence Day. Aunt Elizabeth thought it would help us think of her alive. After all, her soul really is alive, I reminded myself. I suddenly remembered how beautiful Mother looked in July and remembered her humming along with some of the singers. I found the bonnet with the artificial curls made from my hair and helped Aunt Elizabeth put it on Mother's head. I adjusted the curls and began crying uncontrollably. She had been so alive and pretty on Independence Day.

Aunt Elizabeth embraced me, then turned the looking glass to the wall and said, "Remember to hang tea towels over the pictures." She left, promising to return with some food shortly. She turned to Uncle Benjamin in the yard and whispered something to him. I knew she would be telling him to tell Mr. Martin to make a coffin and send for Rev. Boomer from the Second Baptist Church. I shuddered at the thought of putting Mother in a black pine box.

Harriet began to cry in her crib in the next room. Miranda ran to pick her up. She bounced Harriet up and down and said things softly to her and then pinned on a dry clout. Harriet grabbed at the ribbon on Miranda's cap and tried to pull it off, but then seemed to sense that something was different in the house and looked around the room at us all sitting there so solemn. She saw Mother on the bed.

"Mama... Down," she said, and tried to get down and run to Mother. There is no way to tell a year-and-a-half-old baby that her mother has passed on. I began to think about how sad it was that Harriet had never known her father, and now would never know her mother. She would have no memories of Mother singing while she worked, or even of Mother's voice.

Abigail tugged at Mariah's sleeve and motioned that they should help Miranda distract little Harriet. No one wanted to talk. It normally would have seemed nice to have these two quiet for once, but now I missed their noise and activity. Seeing the three of them quietly playing with little Harriet, I asked myself Lucretia's question, "Who will be our mother?"

As if sensing the question in my eyes, Nancy came over to me and patted little Lucretia who was now starting to go to sleep in my lap. "We're going to make it, Betsey. You'll see. But we've got to stay together, don't you think? God will help us. He already provided a job for me at the District School for winter term. I will give you most of what I earn. That will be $1.50 per week. I won't need much since I'll live with the families of the scholars, and I'll come home to visit on Sabbath."

I looked up at her and found it hard to speak, "I-I-I'm not worried about you, Nancy. But I will miss you so much. We've always had each other nearby every day. I can't be the mother here. I'm only twenty years old. I can't imagine keeping up with all the chores and meals and taking care of Harriet. Do you think we would really be allowed to stay together anyway?"

My head began to pound, and I pressed my fingertips hard against the sides of my head, rubbing to try to make the pain stop. I was the oldest now, and I desperately wished I had a solution to our problem. I could imagine Mother's voice, "At your age, Betsey, I was married and had two children." I answered back in my mind, "I'm not you, and I can't do it." *Oh God, what will we do? What will we do? Please help us.*

I heard Jonathan pumping water and looked up to see him through the door, splashing his face and washing the sweat off. Then, cupping his hand, he scooped up a drink. Whenever there was something he had to think hard about, he would go out and split wood for awhile. He had been splitting for a couple of hours now and came in wiping the water from his forehead with his neck scarf.

He came over to Nancy and me and announced, "We've got to stay together. I'll continue to work at my job at the Whitin cotton mill. That will be steady work since they have just built the new brick mill and are doing so well. Nancy has the teaching job starting soon. It's too bad neither of us learned Father's plough-making trade. Maybe we could sell the tools in the shed and the extra ploughs in the barn to Uncle Ellis."

He paused and considered awhile, then rubbing his chin said, "William could learn to make shoes and do that at home in Father's shed. I think Deacon Bachelor would be willing to show him how. I hear it's easy to learn."

He sighed deeply and looked up and around the room awhile, twisting his mouth, and finally said, "Sarah, could probably help him by making the uppers, or I could see if she could work at the mill with me. I don't know. Maybe she should go to school another year or two. Thirteen is such an awkward age for a girl to know what to do. We'll decide that later. Anyway, we could all give our money to keep the family together."

"Abigail and Mariah can continue milking the cows and making themselves useful before school. Miranda could care for Lucretia and take her to school, too, now that she is five." Turning to me, he said, "Or, you could keep her home to entertain Harriet." He didn't mention that I would be getting a job, so I guess he assumed I would stay at home. That is where I want to be.

Nancy and I looked at him in disbelief. "How can you plan all this while you are chopping wood and so soon after Mother died? My mind won't work at all. We should ask Judge Whipple," Nancy said. "Maybe we are crazy to try it."

I couldn't believe my ears. I continued to massage my pounding head. It did actually seem that it could work. We might be able to stay together and no one would be our mother, or all of us would be our mother. Even if it wouldn't work, it gave me hope to think about it now. I got up, laid sleeping Lucretia on the bed in the parlor and came back and gave Jonathan a hug. I was unable to speak, so I just turned and hung tea towels over the pictures. Moving around unsettled my stomach, though, and I ran to the necessary and puked until my stomach felt inside out. Nancy told me to lie down, and she got a cool cloth for my head and helped me to bed.

Jonathan went back outside to find William and Sarah. Since they were old enough to be contributing income for the family, they needed to know the plan, too. In a matter of minutes, they all came back into the house with an expression of firm resolution on their faces. I got up. Yes, we would make it, and Jonathan, Nancy, William, Sarah and I would be the mother. We stood together in a circle near the bed where Mother was laid and put our arms around each other, William joining in reluctantly.

As soon as he joined us, Jonathan prayed simply, "God help us." It seemed as if we were making a promise to God and Mother. Jonathan had told us all the plan, and we all knew what we meant. *Amen.*

I was glad we had had time alone and Jonathan had told us his plan. That was the last time we were alone together until after Mother was buried the next day.

Mr. Martin brought over a coffin and Aunt Elizabeth came back over to help put Mother in it. Sarah brought rosemary and tansy leaves from the garden and sprinkled them over Mother's dress, and then Mr. Martin and Jonathan carried the coffin to the parlor and propped it between two chairs. Sarah followed and sat beside Mother, just looking and looking, talking softly to herself and crying quietly. Nancy put her hand on her shoulder, and the two of them cried. Nobody talked much. Mariah, Abigail, Miranda and Lucretia sat in a circle crying and comforting each other. William went out to the barn and vigorously curried the oxen, talking to them as he did. I went outside, too, and just paced in the yard, rubbing my forehead and temples. I couldn't cry, and my head was splitting and my stomach aching.

Aunt Elizabeth just kept saying "Poor Darlings" and shaking her head. She took our bonnets, removed the colorful ribbons and replaced them with black ribbons and asked if we had dark clothing to wear to the funeral. We determined who did not have anything, and she made a list so she could see if any of the cousins had anything we could use. She gave black arm bands to Jonathan and asked him to give one to William. She asked us not to have the funeral until tomorrow afternoon so she would have time to find mourning clothes for everyone or at least put black ribbons on our bonnets.

Neighbors and friends began bringing food, asking if they could help in any way, saying they couldn't believe it and telling us how much Mother had meant to them. I only half heard them and certainly didn't feel like eating. Jonathan seemed to be the only one to have his wits about him. Olive Nolen, the next-door neighbor who was only a few years older than me, took Harriet and Lucretia home with her.

Rev. Boomer came to read scripture with us and pray. "I'm so sorry about your mother. It doesn't seem possible; she was so healthy until recently. I can't help but think of her lovely voice in the choir in former years. God's ways are certainly not our ways, but God does know what is best. What a blessing it is that your mother was a Christian. You can rest knowing that she will spend eternity with her beloved Savior, Jesus Christ, and will at last see her Samuel and little Silence again. I will see to it that the ladies of the church prepare some food to be served after the funeral tomorrow. Don't you worry about a thing." I could only shake my head; I knew he was right, but I couldn't talk. He said he would be back at the house tomorrow afternoon to pray with us again and lead the funeral procession to the cemetery around the corner where Father and Silence were buried.

Judge Welcome Whipple even stopped in and said he would help us in any way he could. I nodded my head, and wanted to thank him again for being a help to us a few weeks ago by giving us a ride home, but I couldn't say a word; my throat tightened up and my voice wouldn't come. My head hurt so badly. Jonathan told him of our plan to stay together and asked him if it would work. He said he would speak to the other selectmen about it, but thought it probably would work since Jonathan and I were nearly twenty-one, Nancy would have an income soon, and the girls could help around the house.

Nancy, Sarah, Aunt Elizabeth and I stayed up all night to watch with Mother one last time. Sarah didn't want to leave Mother's side. It seemed strange to have her in with us, she who spent most of her time wandering around in a dream world. Nancy told Aunt Elizabeth our plan to stay together, and she seemed to think it would work but was concerned about us especially because of Harriet still being an infant, "poor darling." She said she would talk to Uncle Benjamin and see what he recommended. In some ways I was glad that Judge Whipple and Uncle Benjamin were trying to help us out, but in other ways I just wanted to be left alone so that our family could work out what was best for us. *Oh, God, you are the Father to the fatherless. Please help us. Help me to trust you even when I don't understand your ways.*

The next day, more relatives came. Several aunts and uncles that I had not seen in years came to lay her to rest. I actually was glad to see them but guilty to be happy at a time like this. They were all so kind. Several offered to take some of us home with them. Jonathan told them all our plan, and they were very encouraging. In the afternoon, Rev. Boomer returned. He read some Bible verses about Jesus' return to take believers to heaven, the resurrection of the dead, the new bodies we would have that would never become ill, and assured us again of Mother's profession of faith. We then sang "Why Do We Mourn Departed Friends." The lid was then put on the coffin and a white velvet pall was draped over it. Several relatives carried the funeral bier down the road, around the bend up the next road a half mile, shuffling through the dry brown oak leaves, and up the small hill beside Father and Silence's graves in the Lackey cemetery overlooking the meadow. The fall leaves had been raked away from the place where she was to be buried, and we all gathered beside the grave.

After the prayer in which we were reminded to look at life more seriously and "break away from every enchantment of the world," I left quickly. I couldn't bear to hear the dirt being shoveled onto the top of the coffin. I ran all the way home and went to the barn. Finally the tears came. My chest heaved and I sobbed loudly. William came in and put his arm on my shoulder and just stood beside me. Suddenly, I knew how he felt—he who had taken Father's death so hard. I just wanted to walk away from the house and not go back in to be surrounded by everything that would remind me of Mother. *Oh, God, help us. This is going to be so difficult.*

Sarah and Nancy came in and we hugged each other and cried until the tears wouldn't come any more. Thankfully, the relatives left us alone during this outpouring. The cry did us good. We felt more hopeful and went into the house to hear the relatives tell us all their fondest memories of Mother. It made us cry more, but it felt so good to hear it all.

Grandpa and Grandma Burt were there. They were Mother's parents and had not been well the last few years. We had not seen them at Sabbath meeting for a long time, so I know it was an effort to come to the funeral.

"It should have been me; I'm all done raisin' my family. Poor Tiley wasn't near done," Grandma said. "She was such a good mama to you children. What's to become of you now?" She hugged us all. Grandpa didn't talk but wiped the tears from his cheeks. Mother, their Tiley, was their youngest and now she was gone though only thirty-nine years old.

Sarah seemed to get on quite well with a cousin her age, Prudence, who had come with her parents, Aunt Sarah and Uncle Timothy. They were from somewhere in Bristol County, so she must have been a relative of Father's. There were so many relatives that I had not met before or had met so long ago I didn't remember them. Aunt Elizabeth tried to keep us informed about who all of Father's relations were, but I couldn't keep them straight.

Finally, everyone left but Aunt Elizabeth. Lucretia, Miranda, Abigail and Mariah had been so happy to see all their cousins and were so confident that their older brothers and sisters were going to take care of them, that Mother's death didn't seem to hit them as hard yet. Lucretia and baby Harriet stayed with Mrs. Nolen, and I slept soundly that night for the first time in weeks.

Chapter 6

We Laugh Again
November 21, 1828

    Today, Nancy and I walked down French Road to the long stone wall dam for Job Carpenter's grist mill. We stopped awhile and listened to the water of Great Brook turn the creeking water wheel. There's something solid and beautiful about a stone wall, even if it has a few leaks, as Mr. Carpenter's dam did. And something calming about a brook and waterfall. This was the way we had walked for Mother's burial, and also the way we had started out on our way to the Independence Day celebration last July. Mother was wearing the same dress both days, I mused.

    After sitting in silence awhile, we turned off French Road, following the brook, and walked the half mile more to the little hillside cemetery where Mother, Father, and Silence were buried. We hadn't talked about walking there, but I guess we both wanted to and seemed naturally to turn in that direction.

    It was cold, and a few snow flakes were beginning to fall. We sat on the frosty grass near Father's and Silence's tombstones and Mother's fresh grave and looked over the meadow below. I know Mother doesn't sit here looking out on it, but it is a lovely place to be laid to rest. I wonder if she can see it—the little wild strawberry plants growing everywhere with every vein outlined with white frost, the geese flying overhead trying to decide whether to fly South or not, the sound of the brook flowing through the meadow, and the occasional sea gull gliding by.

"We're making it," I said with a sigh, little puffs of steam forming with every word I spoke. "I couldn't believe how soon they came to make an inventory of the house. The government has to make sure it gets its taxes."

"I know. They wrote down every pot, pan, blanket and spoon we owned," Nancy added. "I admit, though, it made me realize how much we have to be thankful for. I'm so glad harvest is over and we have so much laid up for winter. The barn is full of hay and oats for the cows and oxen. And we have about twenty bushels of potatoes, lots of beans, a tub of meat, and some fresh cider. William is bringing in the last of the corn."

"We have plenty of cash, too," I added, "since all the neighbors who owed* Mother money came and paid instead of waiting until New Years as usual. God is so good to us."

"Of course, we need to get Judge Whipple or someone to help us determine who Mother was indebted to so we can pay them back," Nancy reminded me.

"I know we have a lot to be thankful for, but losing a father and then a mother is hard to bear, and you never get to stop a minute to think," I said. "The sun comes up, the cows need to be milked, meals need to be cooked, and Harriet's at that age when she's getting into everything."

I drew my knees up to my chin, wrapped my long dress around them, and sat in silence awhile, breathing deeply and trying not to cry. A distant crow "cawed" and a dove landed in front of a nearby tombstone and strutted past, mourning softly. Just being quiet and breathing the cool air with Nancy beside me soon had me calm again.

"In no time, Thanksgiving will be over, and you will be teaching in your first District School," I said, putting my arm around her. "I dread your leaving, but I am happy for you. This first year will not be easy. You're hardly older than some of your scholars, Miss Carpenter."

"It will be hard to get used to being called Miss Carpenter," Nancy replied. "I'm glad Dr. Crane introduced me to Rebecca Bradford. She had so much advice to give about first-year teaching since she is new to it herself, and it was good I went with her to the special meeting at Mr. Bennett's house."

"Why? What was it like?"

"I wish you could have heard the Methodist preacher, Rev. Osgood. He is from Providence, Rhode Island, and was the one to get the Northbridge church organized here this summer. They have two nice preachers assigned to them, a Mr. Lovejoy and Mr. Iveson. The church people are all very delightful and so excited about their faith. They have just had a revival, and several men were converted and were talking about it. I've been reading my Bible and praying more since I attended the meeting, not because I feel I should but because I want to know God better. They talk a lot about being holy in your heart and your life. It is wonderful. I have so much more faith in God now, too, and I am even more sure that He will help us."

I stood up and began walking around through the cemetery, breathing deeply and trying to stay calm.

"Nancy, you know I believe God will help us, but I am going to miss you so." I traced the outline of the willow tree on one of the tombstones with my finger, took a deep breath and continued. "I don't think I could bear it if you don't come home on Sabbath, so please don't get too interested in those Methodists. I don't think they could be so different from Baptists; we read our Bible and pray, too, after all. The church people have been so kind to us since...well...you know. I even heard a rumor that the Thanksgiving offering this year is going to be given to us," I told her. "Sarah and I will have more room in bed now, though, which I shan't mind too much except that it will be colder in the winter with just two of us."

"It is good to know I will be missed for such a noble reason," Nancy said as she pinched my side. For the first time in a week, we laughed, and forgot for one brief moment the tombstones beside us. We started to walk home, arm in arm, talking as we walked. Oh, how I wished she were not leaving so soon.

"I'm glad the selectmen agreed that we wouldn't need to be auctioned off. Judge Whipple seems to have taken us under his wing," I said.

Nancy said, "When I go, you need to have a friend your age to confide in. You could probably be good friends with Mrs. Nolen. She is not that much older than you. She's right next door, and her baby Horace is about Harriet's age. You may enjoy taking Harriet over to her house for tea someday when all the children are at school and let them become acquainted. Remember, on the day Mother passed on, she took Harriet and Lucretia to her house."

"That's right. I had forgotten. That does sound like a good idea," I said; "but I am concerned that once you are gone and the children start back to school...well, I'm not sure I can continue caring for Harriet as I should. She still wakes up wet when she naps, and changing her and the straw in her bed all the time and washing the clouts and wet clothes takes so much time. I will need to be doing laundry, baking, sewing, cleaning. I probably won't have time for tea with a friend." I paused to get courage to finish. "I know we said we would stay together, but I'm not sure if it is for Harriet's best for us to keep trying to care for her, and some of the neighbors said they wouldn't mind taking turns caring for her for a few months at a time. It's not as if we'd be splitting up the family, because it is just Harriet and just for a short time."

Nancy stopped walking and seemed almost to stop breathing. She just stared straight ahead and said nothing for a long time. Then, slowly, she let out her breath and blinked a few times, cleared her throat and said weakly, "I suppose if it is for just a few months it would be all right. But what if we start thinking it's too hard and one by one start letting the children go? What if the other children start to worry that you will give them away next? Betsey, please, we must be so careful not to do that, don't you think? And what if one of the neighbors starts acting as if Harriet is theirs and Harriet won't really know who she belongs to?"

I protested. "She wouldn't live that far away, and we could still bring her home occasionally. I just know I don't have the energy to keep up with her, and after all, they offered. Harriet is at that age where she gets into everything. When the children go back to school, there will be no one to entertain her. You know how badly Lucretia wants to be in school; she won't want to stay home to help. I'll try it for awhile, but if I find it too much to handle, don't think me mean. I'll try to get Sarah to help me more, too. She hasn't been so dreamy since Mother died, and really wants to help. I won't say anything to any of the others about it yet. Maybe it will work out better than I think."

"Betsey, thank you for being willing to try. I know I shouldn't expect so much of you when I won't be there to help. You will need the strength of Samson and the wisdom of Solomon, I'm sure," Nancy said. "I'll help you bake lots of pies this next week to last through winter. That will help some."

She's the one that already seemed to be strong and wise, and I found myself wishing for a minute that it was I with the teaching job and she who would stay at home. Then I reminded myself that teaching did not interest me in the least, and I was happiest at home where I could cook and bake and weave and sew. Soon, we would be bringing the loom down from the garret and setting it up, and I did so look forward to that.

We began walking again and Nancy began breathing regularly. We stopped beside the brook near our house and looked up at our little grist mill upstream. The waterwheel was moving slowly creating a kind of music as it turned. I loved its steady rhythm and the whooshing sound it made as the water spilled off it.

"It won't be long before winter," I said, anxious to change the subject, "and it looks as if some of the neighbors are getting some corn ground to meal now before Thanksgiving. They always used to give Mother or Father some of the ground corn as payment for the use of the mill, so I guess they will give it to us now. I shall miss going to the husking bee tomorrow, but I know it wouldn't be proper since we're mourning."

"I'm sure we wouldn't feel like laughing and partying anyway," Nancy said. "I'm just glad we don't need to be all dressed in black for years like Grandma was."

"Nancy, what do you think it will be like for us without parents? I don't want to seem selfish, but do you think any man will be interested in us when we are so needed by the family?" I asked.

Nancy did not have a chance to answer because Miranda and Lucretia who were playing in the apple orchard saw us and came running at us with all their might. "I guess we'll need to talk later, Nancy. It's not a subject I want to talk about in front of the children."

"Betsey! Nancy! I've been playing school with Lucretia," Miranda yelled. Lucretia thought her eight-year-old sister was such a genius to know all those letters and how to read.

"Lucretia," she said, "show Nancy and Betsey how you will recite your ABC's to the teacher when you start school after Thanksgiving. Sit down over there on that log and make believe it is the front row of the girls' side of the school room. I'll be the teacher."

Then Miranda stood up rather straight and tall and, lowering her voice a little and with an air of importance said, "Lucretia, please come recite your ABC's." Then, she quickly ran over and drew a line in the dirt in front of her "teacher's desk" and ran back to her position behind the desk. Abigail and Mariah began to giggle, and she scowled at them, coughed and tapped her stick on her desk.

Lucretia stood up and carefully placed her toes along the line, curtsied, and recited her ABC's, laughing through most of it and then turned around and ran back to her "bench." Nancy and I started to clap, when Miranda called out seriously in her teacher's voice, "Lucretia, where are your manners? You were told to toe the line, curtsy, recite, then curtsy again and wait for the teacher to tell you if your recitation was correct. You forgot to curtsy at the end and wait for my response. Now, come up here and do it again."

Lucretia looked as if she might cry so Miranda said in her usual voice, "We're just making believe, Lucretia. Come on, you can do it." Lucretia shyly got up, toed the line once more, curtsied, said her ABC's in all seriousness, curtsied again, and started to run back to her log seat. We all began coughing, and then she remembered to wait for the teacher's comment.

Miranda realized Lucretia was very nervous by now so commended her highly.

We all then clapped and Lucretia ran to us and grabbed our knees. I picked her up and said, "Lucretia, I can see you are ready to start school with Miranda when Winter Term begins after Thanksgiving. Let's celebrate by…ummm…eating an apple." Each of us found an apple on the ground to eat. William had done a good job of picking most of them last month, though. We ate our crisp, cold apples with a flourish acting as if this were a grand celebration.

"Miranda, I'm so proud of you for teaching Lucretia and reading to her, too! The teacher will be pleased that you didn't forget everything you learned this summer," Nancy said. "Practicing with Lucretia helps you remember."

Miranda smiled brightly. "I wish you could teach at our District School, Nancy."

"The position was not open, Miranda. Maybe someday," Nancy replied.

Abigail and Mariah came running over, both yelling, "The chickens are drunk. The chickens are drunk."

"What do you mean?" I asked.

"Sarah threw out the cider because it was all bubbly, but she didn't want to waste it, so she gave it to the chickens," they said.

We all had a good laugh watching the chickens wander around the barnyard, unable to walk in a straight line.

"Is it a sin for chickens to get dwunk?" Lucretia asked in all seriousness, and we all laughed again until our sides ached.

Thank you for laughter, Lord. A month ago, I wondered if I would ever laugh again.

Chapter 7

Thanksgiving 1828

We all went to the Thanksgiving service at Second Baptist meeting house in the morning. The choir sang beautifully and Rev. Boomer reminded us all to be thankful for our country and do what we could to make it even better. William had invited Cyrus Delaney, the young Irish man who worked on the canal. They had become quite friendly. Cyrus hesitated to go to a Protestant service and seemed uncomfortable sitting inside. He explained that he wasn't a very devout Catholic and had not been able to go to Mass since he had come to the United States, but he had never before been in a Protestant meeting house, and knew he really wasn't supposed to go.

Jonathan talked to Rev. Boomer last week, and told them not to give the Thanksgiving offering to us, because our needs were being met even though we had no parents. He wanted the offering to go to those who were truly needy.

We went to Aunt Elizabeth's and Uncle Benjamin's in Northbridge for dinner and took Cyrus along. We insisted on bringing some food, and I was very proud of the variety of foods that we all managed to make ready in the previous days. Even Sarah had helped by peeling apples for the pies.

William shot a wild turkey using Jonathan's musket. We all were amazed he found one! There was so little wildlife because of all the cleared land and farms around. He took it to Aunt Elizabeth's yesterday, and she cooked it in her new reflector oven.

We made squash pie, apple pie, cranberry tart, pickles, and breads. Next year, I will be daring and try Mother's Marlborough pie. We all missed that tangy lemon taste. I found myself thinking and organizing like a mother. I already felt like a married woman, without one essential ingredient, however—a husband.

Of course Aunt Elizabeth had also baked and made preserves and plum pudding so the table was heaped high. After Uncle Benjamin prayed, Jonathan asked to offer a prayer of thanks "to the giver of all good" for the bountiful table. He thanked God for the memories of those who could no longer celebrate Thanksgiving with us but whom we missed very much. A lump came to my throat and tears to my eyes. We missed Mother, but each day had been so full and busy, that we hardly had time to think of it. After dinner we played games and ate more pies, though I don't know where we fit another bite.

The young men enjoyed a game of rounders, and we women cheered. Cyrus hit the ball quite hard and all three of the young men on the bases were able to run to home where they each scored a point. I found myself cheering wildly for him. The fact that I had seen him work on the canal, and that he had worn the pantaloons I had sewn made me feel as if I knew him well. With his amiable Irish spirit, he was even able to get William to participate in rounders. It was so good to see him running and smiling again.

"Congratulations. You are the hero of your team, Cyrus," I said shyly when they finished.

"It was your cheerin' that made my feet to fly. I didn't know the power of your lungs," he said in his charming Irish accent.

I could feel myself turn red and wondered if I would ever be able to hold a conversation with a young man without blushing.

"I'm sorry I made you to be a-blushin', Betsey, but you are even a prettier lass with a little color on your face, me thinks," he said.

That only made me redden the more, and the whole rest of the day I blushed every time I looked at him. William noticed, and it even made him smile. I was surprised that Cyrus didn't pay much heed to Nancy, and I realized this was the first time I had heard someone say I was pretty.

He was so nice, but I was determined not to become interested, because he had no home or steady income and he was a Papist. I knew my parents would never have approved of me marrying a Roman Catholic.

Now that the canal was finished, the Irish were looking for jobs. Their reputations preceded them, though. Cyrus told us that many employers put signs on their doors reading, "IRISH NEED NOT APPLY!" Jonathan thought he could get him a job at the Whitin cotton mill, though. Everyone knew the Irish could work harder than anyone at physical labor. Mr. Whitin, the owner, was very strict about temperance and would not tolerate workers getting drunk even on weekends. The Irish would need to change their habits if they expected employment there. Cyrus assured Jonathan that he did not drink rum except when working on the canal.

Nancy and I walked around the yard a bit and happened to overhear a conversation between Cyrus and William. Though it was good to see William holding a normal conversation with someone, we distinctly overheard them mentioning going west with some of the families in Sutton who were leaving next spring. I told Nancy about my previous conversation with William this summer when he said he felt the need to leave home and go somewhere far away from the daily reminders of Father's death. We realized that William needed to think this through himself and make his own decision about it. We determined not to bring it up, however, and resolved to make him more content at home.

Lucretia and Miranda were twirling around playing Hen Coop and Chickens and Mariah and Abigail were playing The Graces, sending their barrel hoops high in the air and then catching them with their sticks. They never tired of those silly games. I was glad it was such a pleasant day for November. It could have been May. I was surprised to see Sarah holding Harriet, talking constantly. She must have discovered that babies listen to idle talk about as well as chickens and oxen, and she enjoyed carrying her around describing everything they went past.

Nancy and I went into the parlor to talk with Uncle Benjamin and Aunt Elizabeth and our older cousins. Aunt Elizabeth said, "I must say, I am amazed at how you poor darlings have done since your mother's passing. My, my, it was bad enough to have my poor brother, Samuel, laid to rest two years ago. Your poor mother suffered so from that. I dare say, Doctor Robinson was right in thinking she died from sorrow of mind. But you children seem to be doing quite well."

"Some of us are hardly children any more," I answered. "Jonathan, Nancy and I are past the age that Mother was when she got married, after all." I couldn't believe my ears. The very phrase I hated to hear Mother say had now come out of my own mouth.

"Don't you hesitate to call on us at any time," Uncle Benjamin added. "No one expects you to be independent, you know. We are family, and now that our children are grown, we certainly have time to help you out, and willingly. I only wish we lived closer by. I know William does not want to carry on his father's plough-making enterprise, but if he would like to apprentice to me, I would happily teach him all I know about blacksmithing through the winter months when there is no farming."

"Thank you for your offer, Uncle Benjamin," Nancy said. "We will talk to William about it, but I think right now we need his help with the daily chores of bringing in water, chopping wood, mending fences, and feeding the oxen since Jonathan is working at the cotton mill and doesn't have time for much of that any more. William had a very handsome crop of apples last month."

"Well, perhaps I could just give him a few pointers instead of a full apprenticeship. He might want to do a little blacksmithing on the side some day," Uncle Benjamin said.

"You are so kind, Uncle Benjamin. I miss having you come around all the time as you did when Father was alive. I will encourage William to talk to you about it sometime. Right now, he is enjoying the company of Cyrus Delaney. Cyrus is looking for work now, and he is very strong and a good worker. William worked with him on the canal for awhile," I said. "Perhaps Cyrus would be interested in an apprenticeship." I knew I was blushing even talking about him but hoped Uncle Benjamin hadn't noticed.

Uncle Benjamin coughed a bit and then said, "He's Irish, isn't he?" He laughed and added, "Of course, I know he is."

"Well, yes, he is, but he is a good worker, friendly, and kind. Not everything you hear about the Irish is true. And what is true is not always their fault." I told Uncle Benjamin what William and I had seen when we watched them building the canal. Later when Uncle Benjamin talked with him, he was won over by Cyrus' amiable spirit. He even invited him to stay at their house awhile. What a wonderful way to end a Thanksgiving Day. *Thank you, Lord.*

Uncle Benjamin put some hay in his wagon, and we all got in, and he gave us a ride home. Nancy got her things together so that Uncle Benjamin could take her over to stay at the home of one of the scholars who attend her new school. Jonathan, as usual, had a package. In it were a new quill, a package of ink powder, and one of the new Webster's dictionaries that he bought for Nancy at the company store. He always knew what to get. I gave her a new fancy collar that I had made for her to wear with her dresses. We hugged as if we would never see each other again. None of us rode along because Uncle Benjamin would not have time to take her to Northbridge and bring us all home again before dark. The sun was already starting to set, and when it was dark, the bumpy roads seemed even worse.

I was still so happy from a good Thanksgiving Day, that the impact of her leaving didn't hit me until after she was gone.

William and Jonathan lay a fire while I helped the children get ready for bed. The house was so empty without Nancy there. We all noticed it, even Sarah, who changed Harriet's clout and put her in the trundle bed next to Lucretia. She lay down next to them awhile to keep them warm and I heard her quietly singing to them. It reminded me so of Mother; my eyes welled up with tears and my throat tightened. I must remember in the morning to suggest that she attend the singing school in the spring.

Abigail, Mariah and Miranda got themselves to bed without a fuss. It seemed as if we all had to quietly adjust to the absence of Nancy. I sat by the fire for a long time thinking about how different life was for us in less than two months' time. Mother had died, Nancy had left, and then I remembered Cyrus Delaney and smiled and blushed.

Chapter 8

A Cold Winter Begins
December 1828

"What do you think of Andrew Jackson being elected President?" Olive Nolen asked me one day when I went over with little Harriet for tea. We kept one eye on Harriet and Horace playing on the floor while we talked.

"I suppose I should be interested more in the affairs of our nation, but it didn't seem as if either candidate was worthy of the position, from what I could tell," I answered. "Neither one had much regard for the Sabbath; that sets a poor example for a president." Actually, I never thought about it and was just mimicking what I had heard Mother say. "We will have to wait until March when he is inaugurated to tell anyway. There is so much going on at home, I don't have time to think about such things."

"It has been unbelievably cold and stormy already, and winter has only just begun," Olive continued. "They keep needing to close the Blackstone Canal because the river freezes over. What will January and February be like?"

"The worst part of the weather for me is that Nancy has only been able to come home for one Sabbath since she began teaching, and now Jonathan moved in with someone in South Northbridge. He said it's a nice brick house that Mr. Whitin built especially for the workers, and it's near the mill so he doesn't have to walk so far home in the cold and dark. He used to come home so exhausted after getting up early in the cold dark winter mornings, walking two miles to work, working twelve hours, and then walking home in the dark and cold again. I can't blame him for deciding not to come home at night," I said, "but I miss him."

"I can well imagine you miss them so, and you must be feeling the burden of keeping the family together," she said.

"I miss Nancy and Jonathan more than Mother. Mother, I know cannot come back, but Nancy is so close by, yet I haven't seen her in weeks. And Jonathan is just so stable. I looked forward to his arrival home at the end of the day even though he was too tired to lift a finger," I said.

"We've changed our sleeping arrangements, too," I continued. "Sarah and I have moved into Mother's room to help keep Lucretia and Harriet warm. William now sleeps in the parlor by the fire. Since Jonathan isn't at home anymore, he would freeze to death if he slept by himself in the garret. Miranda, Mariah and Abigail are still up there and it is bad enough for them, but three in a bed is much better than one. We have moved their bed close to the chimney and put blankets over the windows. It makes it dark up there, but at least it is a little warmer. Their faces are rosy when they come down for breakfast. They hate to get out of their bed in the morning because the air is so cold, but the fire going in the kitchen finally lures them. I can hardly wait for winter to be over, and it has just begun."

"You're really the only adult at home now, Betsey. No wonder you feel overwhelmed," Olive said. "I'm just so glad we've become friends. You're such good company for me, and I so look forward to your visits," she said as she bounced little Horace upon her knee. "We have opposite problems. My house is empty all day, and I have no one to talk to. Mr. Nolen isn't much for conversation at the end of the day, either, so sometimes I feel that I will burst if someone won't listen to me."

I put Harriet on my knee and started reciting "Trot, trot to Boston; trot, trot to Lynn; trot, trot to Salem and home again." Olive had me repeat the rhyme until she got it right. Harriet and Horace arched their backs and squealed with delight. The laugh was contagious, and Olive and I were soon joining them. Since I was the oldest, I had said these rhymes to many children already.

"Most of the time Harriet seems like such a burden to me," I said. "I'm glad for these times with you and Horace, but Olive, I don't know if I can keep going all winter taking care of her. I have nightmares that she will crawl into the fire. She isn't happy in her child tender* very long, and she fusses. When the children are at school, I am so busy trying to prepare meals and keep up with sewing, I don't have time to keep her happy. So, she cries a lot."

"You feel all the weight, because you're home all day and have so much to do to keep the family together," she said. "And winter is especially hard. Rachel Prentice has confided in me that she would dearly love to have the baby for a few months. You try to do too much. Remember, you're only twenty years old, and no one expects you to be a mother of nine children."

"Well, Nancy, William, Sarah and Jonathan are hardly children. There are only five young ones, and all but Harriet are fairly independent," I reminded her.

"Still, it's a big responsibility," she insisted.

"I wanted to try to keep the family together, and Nancy wanted me to try hard to keep Harriet. It would be such a relief not to have the responsibility for just a few months, though," I said. "You give me courage. I'll talk to Rachel Prentice about it when I see her at meeting on the Sabbath."

Harriet had been sitting still on my lap until now but turned around, grabbed at my face and said, "Mama."

"She calls all of us Mama," I said. "Even William and Jonathan. I guess we are all parents to her in a way."

"Be sure to let the others help you more. Maybe you should have Sarah stay home from school more often," she added.

"Sarah does stay home to help me on days when I do laundry or baking. And school has been canceled many days because of the snow and cold weather, so then everyone is home. Our house seems really small then. The girls start arguing, and William becomes sullen and resentful with a house full of girls. I'm afraid winter brings out the worst in us. Last week, the girls kept fighting over who got to hold a little stray kitten that had come to our door. After five minutes of screaming on Abigail and Mariah's part, William went over and roughly snatched the kitten from them and threw it as hard as he could out in the snow. The poor thing died, so then the girls were mad at William but afraid to say anything. He felt bad, too, of course, but was fed up with the noise, so there was a sickly quiet in the house for a few days after that."

"You don't have to convince me you need help. Now, don't change your mind about talking to Mrs. Prentice. Both you and Harriet would benefit. Mrs. Prentice adores babies," she said. "Of course that is not going to solve the problem of brothers and sisters being peevish."

Harriet coughed a little, and I cringed. *Dear God, please don't let her die, too.*

Olive seemed to sense my concern. "Don't you worry about that little cough, Betsey. Harriet is fine and just has a cold. You really need to get out of the house more. Bundle up and come over and have tea as often as you like and bring some sewing along. We'll have a good time. I'm sure you are not up to attending the Ladies' Charitable Society yet, but socializing with me would be good for you. By the way, did you hear that some of the people in Uxbridge and Mendon are celebrating Christmas? Some of the people were even staying home from work for it," she added.

"That's ridiculous," I said. "No one even knows for sure when Jesus was born. I thought people came to America to get away from all the foolishness and religious trappings of Great Britain. Why do they want to start it up again here?"

"I don't know, but I did hear that some people are cutting down evergreen trees and decorating them with candles, and it's supposed to be quite lovely," she said.

"I can well imagine it is just an excuse for more frivolity and drunkenness, which this world already has enough of," I said.

I suddenly sounded to myself like a mother out visiting with friends but was reminded that I was missing "the essential ingredient" of a husband. My thoughts turned to Cyrus briefly, and then I reminded myself that he was a Papist, and I forced myself to think of other things.

The wind began to blow, and I decided to head for home now before a full storm came again. I covered Harriet head to toe with a heavy woolen blanket and held her close to me and said my good-byes to Olive and Horace. I put my face down in the blanket and squinting my eyes nearly shut, opened the door and faced the storm. Harriet clung to me, and I wondered how I could be so cruel as to want to give her to someone else to care for. I hurried home as fast as I could.

I could hear William hammering in the addition to the house that used to be Father's plough-making shop. He had decided against blacksmithing, though Cyrus had stayed awhile with Uncle Benjamin and learned a few things. Deacon Bachelor from Northbridge had taught William how to bottom shoes and brought him several dozen pairs a week. It was a good job for a young man who didn't know what he wanted to do in life yet. He also showed Sarah how to sew the uppers, which she worked on when the days were too cold to go to school. How times had changed. When I was their age, Deacon Bachelor used to come door-to-door with his shoe-making kit and make shoes for us in our home, and he would throw in lots of singing for free. Now, it was all sale shoes made for who knows whose feet. I couldn't help but wonder what other things would change in the next few years.

Sarah and William enjoyed each other's company though they seldom spoke much. Sometimes she would read books to him that she borrowed from the schoolmaster. William had had a difficult time with reading in school, but he loved to hear a story read aloud. They both enjoyed the frontier tales of James

Fennimore Cooper and the homey stories of Catharine Sedgwick. I tried to listen in or sometimes would have Sarah sit in the doorway between the shop and the house so I could hear her. I was afraid the frontier tales would make him want to leave home all the more, though.

William had been right about the girls not helping much around the house. My winter plan was to correct that. Miranda continued to keep Lucretia occupied, so I began teaching Abigail and Mariah how to sew. Thankfully, we didn't milk through the winter, because the cows were going to calve in the Spring, so we turned our energy from milking, cheese and butter-making to sewing. I showed them how to make heavy quilted petticoats out of old dresses. Having all those layers of cloth on their laps helped keep them warm.

I had William bring the loom down from the garret, too. It took me days to thread the warp threads through the loom, but then it was ready to make toweling. There was nothing I loved better than weaving, though toweling was rather boring. I preferred the more complicated patterns for woolens, but there was no sense making them now. The power looms made better cloth, and so much faster. They even had steam-powered looms in Rhode Island, I heard. On cold afternoons, I pushed the loom closer to the fire and got a good steady rhythm going. Weaving helped keep me warmer.

When Harriet was awake, I would keep her in the baby-tender until she fussed, and then I would tie one end of a rope around her waist and the other end to the loom so she couldn't get into the fire. She was walking quite well now so I had to be very careful with her. She learned to use the little child-sized potty. I think she discovered how uncomfortable it was if she had a wet clout freezing on her, and determined to keep dry. I hoped the weather would improve enough for us to attend Sabbath meeting so I could ask Mrs. Prentice if she were still willing to take Harriet home for a few months. It had been too cold to walk the 45 minutes it took to get to the meeting house the last couple of Sabbaths, and that made the winter seem even longer.

Some days were bitter cold. I was glad our necessary was in the wood shed and not out back like some of the neighbors. Poor William had to go outdoors to feed and water the livestock and Sarah would bundle up and help him. Wrapping wool scarves around their necks, heads and faces, leaving only their eyes showing, they trudged out onto the squeaking snow. The water would freeze almost as soon as they poured it in the trough. When they came in, frost lingered on their eyelashes and eyebrows and even in their noses. They rubbed their hands together briskly, holding them up to their faces and blowing to try to warm them. The house wasn't much warmer than the outdoors. We had a rule that every time anyone used the necessary or went to the root cellar, they had to bring more wood in to the house. That meant there were fewer times the door would need to open.

I took advantage of the need to have a hot fire going and cooked up most of the pumpkins in a kettle, then mashed them, spread them in tin plates and put them in the warming oven to dry. I read that hint from Olive's copy of *The American Frugal Housewife*. Now, when I want some pumpkin for vegetable or pie, I just break off a piece and boil it up in milk.

Other days, when it was too cold to go to school, I had William bring up apples from the root cellar. I sliced them thin, and the little girls strung them in front of the fireplace to dry. They made the house smell glorious and provided a chewy treat throughout the winter.

Olive told me the newspapers said it was the coldest winter we had had in years. Keeping fires going in the house kept us very busy and seemed to do so little good. Any water we left around in bowls froze, and the wet dish cloths were like boards. The frost on the windows was so thick, we couldn't see out. Sometimes the girls would scratch designs in it with their fingernails. A heavy layer of solid ice framed each window.

When it wasn't too cold to be out, William would hitch the oxen to a sleigh and go collect firewood from the woods. The girls would go along for the sleigh ride and help him when they weren't too busy having a snowball fight or making snow angels.

Chapter 9

Lucretia's Birthday
January 18, 1829

    Jonathan and Nancy made a point of coming home this afternoon because it was Lucretia's sixth birthday. Jonathan handed her a package, tightly tied. In her effort to pull off the string, she hit herself in the mouth and knocked out her first tooth. She looked as if she were going to cry when she saw the tooth in her lap.
    "Well, I guess you are growing up after all, Lucretia. You're losing your baby teeth. Let's see you smile," Jonathan said. "Look at that. You have a grown-up tooth coming in its place already. Look everybody."
    We all "oohed" and "aahed" and finally Lucretia decided losing the tooth was a good thing after all, and she smiled.
    "Open the package, Lu," Miranda reminded her.
    Lucretia opened it and held up some pretty blue calico fabric, a packet of sewing needles and a pin cushion.
    "Betsey, can Mariah and I make her a dress?" Abigail asked.
    "What a grand idea," I answered. "We can take apart her red dress to use as a pattern. I'll cut it out for you and show you how to sew. You won't believe how many thousands of stitches go in a dress, though. Lucretia could even help with the

hemming with those new needles. I'll let her practice hemming some toweling, and if she does well, she can hem her dress."

Lucretia ran over and hugged me, smiling so broadly. Everyone laughed to see the gaping hole where her tooth had been, and she felt around it with her tongue.

"Whath so funny?" she asked, and surprised herself with her newly acquired lisp. Then she sat there and recited her numbers and ABC's to see which ones sounded different.

We all laughed. We had not laughed in so long that when we finally started, it grew and grew until we were all holding our sides in pain. Jonathan began snorting and Lucretia squealed in delight. She went around to all of us giving us hugs and saying "A-B-Thee" for everyone. Even Harriet joined us in laughing, though her laughs seemed to have question marks on the end as she wondered what it was that was so funny.

Lord, thank you for our family and for simple pleasures.

Nancy helped me put dinner on. We ate early so Jonathan and Nancy would have time to walk back to Northbridge before it was totally dark. It was so good to have other adults in the house. At the table, she told us all about her school experiences as well as her friendship with Rebecca Bradford, the other young teacher who was seemingly converting her to the Methodist ways. I wanted everything to stay as it had been. Why must there be so many changes? I had gotten used to living without a father, but didn't know if I would ever be used to living without a mother. I wished we could go back to Independence Day and keep everything as it was then. Nancy and Jonathan would be home and Mother would be alive. And it would be warm and sunny. I felt so old now. Had it only been six months ago that I was so annoyed at Mother for telling me, "When I was your age, I was married and had a child"? *Lord, forgive me for my pettiness, and help me to cherish the good things I have now.*

Jonathan interrupted my thoughts. "Guess who is working at the mill now?" He looked right at me, and suddenly I knew it must be Cyrus. I started to blush again.

Jonathan noticed. "You guessed it," he said.

"She didn't say anything," Abigail noted. "Who is it?"

Jonathan laughed and told her, "Cyrus Delaney. Remember him from Thanksgiving Day?"

"Of course," she said. She looked at me and giggled.

I avoided her glance and got up to clear the table.

William said, "Maybe you could bring him home sometime so I won't be as outnumbered by all these girls."

The mere mention of Cyrus in the conversation had the same effect on William as having him here. He became warm and cheerful.

"When it warms up in the spring, we'll come Saturday after work and stay for a Sabbath meeting if I can convince him to come in a Protestant building again. Otherwise, he can stay at home, and we could just go for the morning service and come home for nooning and the rest of the afternoon," Jonathan said.

"I fear we will become pagans without the influence of our parents," I said, and a picture of Cyrus flashed into my mind. It was after the game of rounders on Thanksgiving Day, and he had said, "It was your cheerin' that made my feet to fly."

I looked at myself in the looking glass and saw my dry, red skin and cracked lips. I don't think Cyrus would think me a pretty lass now, I said to myself.

Chapter 10

A Visit from Judge Whipple
Early February 1829

    The winter snows had begun in earnest. We had one snowstorm after another, and all of us had to help with shoveling so we could continue getting to the barn, and keep a path shoveled out to the road. Our cheeks, foreheads and chins were all red and chafed from the cold, and each time we came in, the hair that had stuck out from our hats was coated with a thick heavy coating of snow, making us look like rag dolls with frozen thick white yarn for hair.
    One morning our pump was frozen, as was the Nolen's and several other neighbors'. It took us till afternoon to get it thawed. Jonathan came home for a few of those days because the waterwheel froze up at the mill. He and William cut a little firewood, but couldn't stand being out for long. As soon as it warmed up a little, he went back to work at the mill.
    It was hard work to keep warm. Our hands and feet were in pain from the cold when we had been out shoveling for only half an hour. Abigail, Mariah and Miranda, who were so good-natured normally, were crying pathetically because their feet and hands hurt so badly. It was only worse to try to warm ourselves by the fire.
    We all took off our stockings and mittens and soaked our feet and hands in pans of cold water, adding warm water gradually until finally the full bucket was slightly

warm and our body temperature was normal again. Mother had taught us that trick. The whole process was done amidst moaning and sobs and cries and whimpers by all of us, with much shaking about of our hands and feet, trying to deal with the enormity of the pain. We couldn't bear to sit still so we kept standing up and sitting down, trying to keep our balance with our feet in the bucket, alternately sitting on our hands, clapping them, biting them, all the while crying out most bitterly. Meanwhile noses ran, tears streamed down our faces, and we were all a most pathetic sight. Last July, in the summer heat, I had longed for winter. I had clearly forgotten some of the side effects.

Harriet was so fussy now, too. She was getting too old for both a morning and afternoon nap, but couldn't quite make it with one nap. She would fuss because she was sleepy but then wasn't tired enough to fall asleep. Being confined with a fussy child made me nearly lose my mind. I will soon be ready for the lunatic asylum.

One mid-day, in this brutal winter season during a brief lull between storms, Judge Whipple came over and said he needed to talk to me. I invited him in to sit by the fire, happy for an excuse to stop the cleaning I had begun. Most of the others were in the barn thrashing the rye. Lucretia, Harriet and Miranda were playing house in the next room, dressing their little corn cob dolls with scraps of cloth they had sewn into doll clothes.

"Betsey, you and your family have been doing so well since your mother's death. I am amazed that you have been able to keep the family together. Do you think it will continue to work, or should we plan to make some other arrangements?" he asked.

"Does 'other arrangements' mean to be put up for auction at the spring Town Meeting?" I asked softly hoping the girls wouldn't hear me in the next room where they were sewing. "That would be so humiliating and dreadful."

"No, you needn't worry about that, but it more likely would mean selling the property and dividing the inheritance among the heirs and seeing if various relatives would want to take some of you in. Your parents have plenty of family spread all over from Rehoboth to Oakham, not to mention those close by in Douglas and Northbridge. I'm sure many of them would love to have such well-behaved children join their families," he said.

"Well, many of them told me after the funeral that they could take one or two children, Mr. Whipple, but we don't want to split up the family if we can help it. Besides, several of us are hardly children any more. Mother was married and had children when she was my age," I said. There I was again repeating the same phrase I had detested hearing from Mother.

"Betsey, she had a husband who was ten years older than she and a property owner at that, a hard worker with a steady income from his established plough-making business. That is certainly not your situation now. I think if you are determined to stay together, we need to draft a legal document to that effect and take steps to make your financial future more certain. I would like to send Mr. Salmon Burden over to write up such a document, if you don't mind. All of you who are over fourteen years of age could read it, and if you are in agreement, sign it. Then we will need to take a look at the wills. We still have not probated your father's will, so we will do that, too, and then your mother's," he said.

"What would the legal document say, Mr. Whipple?" I asked. "And what does 'probate' mean?" I felt so young and inexperienced all of a sudden.

"I would suggest that the document would read that all of the children between the ages of fourteen and twenty-one would agree to give any money they earn to the family estate. That way, each of you is contributing to the welfare of the family and not saving up money for your own use," he answered.

"Well, that's not a problem. We're doing that anyway. Nancy and Jonathan give us all the money they earn from teaching and working in the cotton mill, keeping only enough out for necessary odds and ends, and William and Sarah give us all the money they get from making shoes. I have no income except some occasional small change from selling extra cheese. There is so much to do in keeping the household warm and fed that I can't be expected to have a job, too," I protested.

"Nobody is expecting you to have a job, Betsey. It would be just a statement that if you did receive any money, it would go to the family. How old are you?" he asked.

"I'll be twenty-one in May. What happens to me after my birthday, then if the document is only for those under twenty-one?" I asked. I pictured myself out in the cold, begging for scraps of food in the town common, but then realized that that would never be allowed, and I for sure would be sold at auction, unless of course I got married. But who would marry me?

Judge Whipple, however, brought me back to my senses by simply saying, "There would be nothing keeping you from putting any money aside for yourself that you earned after you turn twenty-one, and you could ask to have your part of the inheritance. That might involve selling land; I don't know. That will be determined when the will is probated which means settled. We determine who owes your family money and to whom you are indebted and see if you end up with money left over or need to sell property to pay your indebtedness. If your inheritance includes land, you could build on it if you wanted to get married," he added with a twinkle in his eye.

I blushed. "Mr. Whipple, please. No young men have shown any interest, and I am in no hurry to be married. Why does everyone think that a man is such an essential ingredient for happiness? I could remain single and be perfectly happy for some time yet," I said, though I'm not sure I believed it. I started to add that when you're married, you have the obligations of family, but I caught myself just in time from making that stupid remark. Who could have more obligations of family than I with nine children?

"I do think it is time to get something in writing. All of you children will then know what is expected of each other, and the townspeople will realize that something official has been done. I'll write down the names of those of you who are over the age of fourteen if you would be so kind."

"Well, there's me of course, and Jonathan, Nancy and William. Oh my goodness. I just realized William turned fifteen a few days after Mother died, and we never celebrated his birthday. Poor William. Let's see. Sarah will be fourteen in July. Should she sign?"

"No, they must be over fourteen at the time the document is written. I also think it is time your family has a legal guardian appointed. Since you want to try to stay together, I think it best if we appoint a responsible neighbor. Mr. Nolen, I think would be good; though he has only been married a few years and is but twenty-eight years old, he has a lot of business sense. I will talk to some of your relatives in Northbridge, Sutton and Douglas, and see if they object to his appointment since they live at enough of a distance to make their appointment an inconvenience. Your father, I remember, spoke highly of Mr. Nolen. He would have liked to apprentice him into plough-making, but Mr. Nolen was interested in making those gun barrels, and that was that. He has done well, thanks be to God."

"Mrs. Nolen and I are good friends now. I would feel peculiar asking my friend's husband for money. Why don't I just keep the money and handle it?" I asked. "It will be an inconvenience to always need to ask Mr. Nolen for every little thing."

"It may seem inconvenient at times, but in the long run, I'm sure you will come to realize that it will be to your advantage to have your guardian handle finances. As I mentioned, when you are twenty-one, you may keep any money you earn, and in fact you could make charges to the estate for the care of the family," he replied. "At your age, there may be some who would try to take advantage of you as well, and Mr. Nolen would make that much less likely to happen. I'm sure that he would see to it that all was done fairly and would keep everything in order. The fact that he lives next door would also greatly reduce any inconvenience, don't you think?"

"I suppose so."

"Perhaps you could work something out with him to advance you a certain amount for small things that come up, so you wouldn't need to bother him for every little thing, as you say. You needn't think of him as a father; he is more like an older friend, and the fact that you are friends with his wife is to your advantage."

"I suppose so," I repeated, unconvinced, and unready to give up some of the independence that I had been beginning to feel. I then remembered about my conversation with William so many months before. It seemed like years. "What happens if one of us moves away before we turn twenty-one?" I added.

"Well, if he or she moves far away, it is nearly impossible to enforce. It is a legal document, however, and each person who signs it is expected to comply."

"I will talk it over with Jonathan and Nancy next time they come home for Sabbath, if this snow will ever let up for a week-end."

"Very well, then." He stood and put on his hat, bowed slightly and went to the door. He really was such a fine gentleman and was so convincing by just quietly explaining things. "Please let me or Mrs. Whipple know if we can ever be of any service to you and your fine family."

"Thank you, sir, very much. You are too good. I'm sorry if I seem ungrateful or rude. Sometimes I feel so old, independent and responsible, and other times so young and confused. You are a big help to our family. Thank you so much," I said as I let him out the door.

Unbeknownst to us, a blinding snowstorm had started, and he ducked his head into the wind, wrapped his scarf around him and started trudging through the blowing snow toward his home a good half-mile away. He had only gone a few feet when I could see him no longer. The snow made a thick curtain between us.

I shut and latched the door quickly and swept the snow aside that had blown in when the door was opened. I added more wood to the fire, began peeling potatoes and wondered about this latest development and how it would affect us. Harriet began to fuss, and Lucretia quickly picked her up and brought her out to me. It was so nice having Lu at home to help with Harriet. Maybe I should just keep her home from school another year and forget about sending Harriet elsewhere. After all we were a family.

The others came running in from the barn, covered with snow. "We could hardly find the house," they said. William went into the shed and began bottoming shoes.

Only minutes passed before we heard a knocking on our door once again. There was poor Judge Whipple caked with snow and breathing heavily. He looked like a life-sized snowman. He could hardly talk for being so winded but finally managed to say, "I will never make it home. I cannot even tell where the road is. This storm is blinding. Will you be so good as to let me stay here until the worst of it is over?"

"Of course. I am so used to people helping us, I am only too glad to be able to return the favor," I added. "I hope you enjoy stew. I'll add some more potatoes, and you are welcome to stay. Warm yourself by the fire."

"I appreciate your hospitality. While I have my coat on, though, let me go bring in some more wood." He knew right where to go and went out the kitchen door to the woodpile next to the necessary. We heard him out there stomping the snow off his shoes and brushing off his coat from his encounter with the storm. Soon, he was back in again, his arms full of wood which he dropped in the bin near the door.

"That woodpile is getting very low, Betsey. Is William the only one you have splitting wood?"

"Yes, William has done most of it since Jonathan began working at the Northbridge cotton mill. Now, because of the storms, Jonathan hasn't even been home for weekends for a couple of weeks. He usually helped William split wood on weekends; he says it helps him think."

"Well, I don't want to seem critical, but you really need to get more wood in here. Now, this is the type of thing that Mr. Nolen could help you with. He more than likely knows of someone with extra firewood split and could arrange a trade either in goods such as some of those extra plough handles you have in your barn or a promise of William helping with haying in the summer. Mr. Nolen would figure it out."

"I suppose you 're right. William is too shy to approach other neighbors and suggest such a thing."

As if he heard his name, William came in from the other room. "Judge Whipple. I thought I heard you leave," he said in surprise.

Judge Whipple explained about the storm and then very kindly explained his suggestions of guardianship and signing the document to William.

William had the hint of a smile and said, "It sounds like our Declaration of Independence."

"I suppose it is, in a way, William," Judge Whipple answered. "However, you children, ah, rather, young people, must not think that people expect you to be able to do everything yourselves. You not only need the help of your Heavenly Father, on whose name you must not hesitate to call, but also your neighbors and relatives. Though I admire you for wanting to try so hard to keep the family together, doing it may become a type of idolatry, if you don't mind my preaching to you a bit. That is one of the benefits of attending the same place of worship, though. I feel free to give you a little deaconing advice. Though I am a judge, the title I value most is deacon."

He hesitated, looked at his folded hands and began bumping his thumbs against each other. Finally, he looked up and continued, "Keeping the family together at all costs is not necessarily what is best for each family member. You must constantly pray for the guidance of our Lord. His will may well be that you become part of other families. The essential thing is that you do the will of your Heavenly Father. I'm sure your regular attendance at meeting on most Sabbaths under the scriptural preaching of Rev. Boomer has taught you that much." He ran his hand through his thinning gray hair, over the back of his neck, scratched the back of his head and looked at us over the top of his foggy spectacles.

"Yes, we know," I answered. I was a little taken aback that he didn't wholeheartedly support our independence, but had to admit the truth of what he said. "We know," I repeated, "but a reminder from you with your quiet and gentlemanly spirit is a blessing." *Lord, help me not to worship independence as the highest goal. Help me to worship you and remember to ask for your direction.*

Judge, rather, Deacon Whipple stood and looked out the window. He turned back and said, "I don't want to abuse your hospitality, and the storm has let up some. I think I should take advantage of the last bit of light to walk quickly home. My poor wife and aged parents are probably beginning to worry by now. I leave happy that I had the opportunity to talk with your further in more of a Deacon Whipple than a Judge Whipple tone; I think it was Providential. I will keep your family in my prayers and I'll ask Salmon Burden to draft the document I mentioned. God be with you, friends." And, with that, he buttoned his coat and left once again. His addressing us as friends reminded me that someone had told me once that he was of Quaker background. They always call each other "friends."

Thank you, Lord, for Friends.

Chapter 11

Our Declaration of Independence
Mid-February 1829

There were now three feet of snow on the ground, and in many places it had drifted to five or six feet. Shoveling after the last blizzard was particularly difficult since the snow was so deep. We had to throw the shovels of snow over our heads; we felt as if we were making our way through a tunnel.

William figured out the most efficient way to do the job and insisted that his way would get it done more quickly. He pushed all the snow off to the side of the path first, and then did the lifting and throwing over his head. The rest of us had been lifting and throwing each shovelful. I don't know if he was right, but I was glad to see him have a strong opinion and show some leadership, so I willingly submitted and saw to it the others did, too.

"Everyone clean off the path good. Don't leave any clumps of snow," he called out. "If you do, tomorrow, the clumps will be frozen like rocks and will trip us and be very hard to get up later."

"Look at the roof," I said. "There's a good two feet of snow up there and a solid layer of ice around the edge. The icicles look like fangs on a giant white winter monster."

Winter did seem to be out to devour us. It took all our energies just to keep up with clearing away the snow and making meals. I was a bit envious of people who had stairs inside their houses leading to their cellars. Every time we needed food from the root cellar or barn, it meant going outdoors and shoveling a path. We couldn't keep food in the house because it would freeze. The root cellar was cool, but not freezing.

One day it was so cold we couldn't stay out more than a few minutes, and the next day we awoke and the sun was shining. The ice was melting from the roof. It was so warm, we only had to wear light jackets. The sunshine and warm weather had a magic effect on us. We sprang to life, began singing and running around, making jokes and teasing each other. It was as if a heavy veil had been lifted or we had been let out of a cage. People ran out of their houses and went to neighbors' houses yelling out "Hellos" and were generally very cheery.

We saw Deacon Whipple, and he made an appointment for all of us over the age of fourteen to meet with him on Saturday afternoon to sign the document that Mr. Burden had prepared. If the warm weather does hold, Jonathan and Nancy will come home for the week-end after working a half day on Saturday.

With warm weather came a resolve to finish projects we had begun. Evenings, when the girls were home from school, we finished the dress for Lucretia, each of us sewing some part of it, including Lucretia herself who helped with the hemming. Mariah and Abigail made the cuffs for the sleeves, all of them helped with the straight seams, and I did the collar and the puff sleeves. Miranda and Lucretia kept getting knots in their thread and caught pieces of cloth into their sewing that didn't belong, so they had to rip them out, but we made an effort to make light of their mistakes. It took us several days, but we were enjoying it so much, the time passed quickly. With so many girls in the family, we had our own sewing society. Sarah continued helping William with shoes during the day. At night, she would read to us by candlelight while we continued to stitch. Thankfully, Harriet went to bed early. During the daytime, when the girls were in school, she was a handful. She was talking more and becoming stubborn. Her favorite word was "no."

After a few days of bright sun and thawing, puddles and flooding became the problem. There was nowhere for the water to go. The ground was still covered with some snow and was quite cold and hard, so the melted snow created small ponds in the paths we had so carefully shoveled a few days ago. Getting to the barn or out to the neighbors was almost impossible. The only way to go was to trudge through the snow that hadn't melted yet. It was quite wet, so any trip out of the house meant a change of clothes when we returned or else standing for hours by the fireplace to dry. I did the laundry for the first time in a month because there was finally the hope of clothes drying quickly outdoors. We laid the wet clothes over shrubs and the bare tree limbs to dry. During the cold spell, anything we had hung to dry in the house had frozen stiff as a board and dried gradually. Hanging clothes outside in the sun was such a blessing. They smelled so good when we brought them in. If the warm weather should continue, I may even wash my hair. I think it was before Thanksgiving when I washed it last.

Thankfully, the sloppy roads did not prevent Jonathan and Nancy from coming, and we went to Judge Whipple to sign the document. It read,

> "We the Subscribers, minors above the age of fourteen years, and children of Samuel Carpenter, late of Sutton deceased, do hereby agree to remain in and labour in, and for the support of our Father's family, and turn the profits of our labour in, as common stock into our said Family, during minority. Signed in the presence of Welcome Whipple, Salmon Burdon, Samuel Cofman."

Also, that day, George Nolen was appointed by the selectmen to be our guardian. Having these things so official should have made us feel more secure, but I no longer felt in control and I wasn't sure I liked it. I wanted to talk to Olive about it.

We were finally able to get to Sabbath meeting the next day. Rachel Prentice came over to see how we were doing. She asked if she might hold Harriet, and Harriet went right to her and was fascinated by the artificial curls on her bonnet. They must have reminded her of Mother. "I would be so happy to take little Harriet home with me, Betsey, wouldn't I, Harriet," she said, bouncing her up and down. Harriet seemed to like her very much, and I found myself ready to cry. "I have plenty of clouts around yet from when my children were babies. I miss having a baby around the house, don't I, Harriet; you sweet little darling. You think about it, Betsey. Harriet and I would get along just fine, wouldn't we?" She gave Harriet back to me, and Harriet seemed hesitant to leave her.

I thought of my conversation with Nancy in the fall and then of my conversation with Olive in the winter. "You can't start giving away the children," Nancy said in my mind. "You can't do it all yourself," Olive replied. I looked up at Mrs. Prentice, in a confused state of mind and told her I would think about it.

Nancy and I talked on the way home from meeting, and she agreed that with warm weather coming and the children being in school for a couple of months yet, it would be all right to let Harriet stay with Mrs. Prentice for awhile.

Chapter 12

Family Matters
March 1829

    I visited Olive today for tea. My troubled state must have been obvious because she asked if something was bothering me.

"I feel very peculiar about your husband being our guardian. We were getting to be good friends, and I don't want you to think of me as a daughter," I confessed.

"Don't be silly," she said. "I am not your guardian. Mr. Nolen is. He takes care of me, too, and I don't think of him as a father. He has a lot of business experience and is older than we are and is an honest man, so you can trust him to make sound decisions and be a help to you. I'm sure you will soon be glad that he is willing to help you in this way."

"I don't know how to talk to him, though. He is never home when we visit, and I just feel so awkward. You must help me, Olive. I don't feel like I am in control any more. Here I am old enough to be married myself and yet I need to ask permission from a neighbor for things."

"Betsey, you are making much ado about nothing. Remember when you talked of letting Mrs. Prentice take care of Harriet for you? If you still decide to do that, I'm sure it will be far less embarrassing to have Mr. Nolen reimburse her out of the estate than for you to do so. And, if you find you need help with ploughing or planting or harvest, Mr. Nolen can do the hiring and paying for you, which at your age, I don't think you will want to handle anyway. If you need supplies, you need never feel shy about asking Mr. Nolen because he is your appointed guardian. If he weren't appointed, you would feel hesitant to ask him very often. Don't you see what an advantage it is? And I will invite some of you over for dinner very soon so you can meet my dear husband on a social level and see what a good man he is. Your father liked him very much, and I am sure you will, too. Now stop being such a silly goose, and let's drink our tea and talk about our babies as usual."

"Olive, what would I do without you? You have become like an older sister to me, and to tell the truth I never liked being the eldest in my family, so I feel relieved of the position. Now, I need your advice. You may have noticed a young man at our house on a couple of occasions. He is a friend of William's and now Jonathan's. He is Irish and William met him working on the Blackstone Canal. Now he works at the Whitin cotton mill with Jonathan. He is very nice and polite and hard-working—not at all fitting the description we hear of the loud, swearing, drunken Irish. He is, of course, a Papist by birth but has not had the occasion to attend Catholic services for years. He, um, seems somewhat interested in me. That is, only mildly so, of course. We haven't spoken together or seen each other except when with family, but he has commented to William about me. And I just wondered what you thought."

"Betsey, all of the sudden I am not feeling very wise. Matters of the heart are so hard to be rational about. Sometimes I think it was not such a bad idea to have match-makers since love can be so blind. If our lives were as simple as fairy tales, you could just marry no matter what and live happily ever after."

"Olive, please, I said he was only mildly interested in me. He is not talking to me of marriage," I said.

"I know, but relationships with young men are not worth pursuing if they do not lead in that direction. Men are not pawns for women to play with and put away after the game is over. Do not waste time on a relationship that does not have the potential to end in marriage. You and he will only hurt one another."

"Are you saying that I should not encourage this young man in any way, then?" I asked.

"I know you value your faith very much and agree with the teachings of your church," she added quietly. "Perhaps you should talk with your minister about this since this young man is a Papist."

"There is no sense talking to him since there is no relationship. Besides, I know what he would say because he had a sermon about other religions right after I met

Cyrus—that's his name. He told us that papists place as much emphasis on what the church and the Pope say as they do on what the Holy Bible says. But sometimes it seems that we do the same thing. We always ask about what our church thinks, not what the Bible teaches," I said sadly.

"If you two ever did want to get married, who would marry you? Your minister surely would not, and the Justice of the Peace is a Deacon in your church so he surely wouldn't either. It seems to me this relationship does not stand a chance. You would have to be very convinced it was worth fighting for if you pursue it. You are young yet, though. I know your mother used to always tell you she was married at your age, but most of our generation is waiting longer to marry, and I wouldn't set your hopes on the first young man that shows interest," she said.

"I know almost nothing about Cyrus and so it is silly for me to allow my imagination to get carried away. Since Mother and Father died, I really want someone stable to provide for me, and I am afraid I am jumping at the first possible candidate instead of using my head," I said.

"How old is Cyrus?"

"I don't know. He looks to be about my age."

"A young man of your age with a job at the mill is probably not in a position to provide for you, Betsey, especially if he is Irish. He wouldn't own property and has no family around to help. My husband is five years older than I and was already established in a business before he approached me," she said.

"I will try to use good judgment. I am so glad I talked to you. Please don't mention it to anyone, though, not even Mr. Nolen, even though he is my guardian, because as I said, there is nothing in this relationship yet anyway."

"I will not tell a soul," she said.

"And Olive, I do think I will let Mrs. Prentice take Harriet for awhile," I said, my eyes welling up with tears. "Judge Whipple said the best things aren't always the easiest. If the weather is still warm, I will take her there tomorrow, and if she seems happy, I will leave her for awhile."

Olive came over and put her hand on my arm. "I know it will be hard for you, but I think Harriet will enjoy the mothering that Mrs. Prentice will have time to give her."

Harriet looked up at us from one to the other and saw that I was crying. She patted my chest and offered me her favorite blanket. I hugged her tightly, and told Olive I needed to go home for a good cry.

I went back home just before the girls arrived home from school at half past four. It is such a long day for them in the winter when they don't come home for nooning. Miranda came running up to me and whispered in my ear, "Abigail and

Mariah's friend Chloe was teaching them to dance today after nooning." It almost took my breath away. How could they do that?

"Abigail and Mariah, come here this minute. Miranda tells me that you are learning to dance at school. You know Mother and Father would not approve, nor does our church allow it. I'm shocked at you and ashamed."

Abigail and Mariah glared at Miranda and she looked down at the floor, pursed her lips together tightly and walked away awkwardly, saying, "Well, you did, and you know it."

Abigail said, "I don't know what is so wrong with it. It's just the quadrille and such fun. You stand in lines facing each other, and…"

"I know what it is," I said. "I am not so old that I don't know what is going on in the world. You hold hands with a young man, though, don't you?"

Mariah said, "Yes, but it's not like that awful waltz where you keep holding on to a boy and face each other for the whole dance. It is really very fun."

"Well, holding hands with young men is not appropriate when you are not even courting. You know Mother and Father would never allow such amusements. Once you allow the quadrille, it won't seem like such a big step after all to the shameful waltz. I won't allow it. I don't want to hear of it again, do you understand?" I said.

"Yes, I understand what you are saying, but I don't agree," Abigail answered.

"If I hear of you doing it again, you will not be allowed to stay at the schoolhouse for nooning. You will need to walk home no matter how cold it is. You must learn to do what is right," I said. "I don't understand why the schoolmaster would allow such a thing when they are so careful to keep the boys from the girls in the classroom. First thing you know, they will allow boys and girls to come in through the same door and sit next to each other in school," I said.

Abigail said, "Betsey, you know that would never happen. The quadrille is just like a game only with music playing. You just don't understand."

At that, she and Mariah stomped out of the room and up the stairs to their bedchamber, grumbling the whole way. Miranda came over and whispered in my ear, "The schoolmaster don't know about it. They do it out of his sight."

Lord, help me to do what is right in your eyes, but not to make them bitter.

That night after I put Harriet to bed, I told the girls my plan to take Harriet to Mrs. Prentice's house tomorrow. This announcement was adding insult to injury. First, I wouldn't allow them to dance, and now I was giving away their sister. They protested violently, and I realized my timing had been all wrong, but now the deed was done. I had prayed, but I had not listened for an answer.

Sarah did her best to calm them down, and they went to bed early. I listened calmly for God's answer. I heard no words, but when Sarah and I talked later, I knew what to do. We decided the girls should stay home from school the next day. In the morning, we discussed the reason for making the decision, and they saw that I did not want to give Harriet away but thought this temporary solution was best. They helped me pack up some of her clothes and we all went together to take a walk to Mrs. Prentice's. We agreed that if Harriet was terribly unhappy, we would not leave her there.

Mrs. Prentice saw us coming and came out to greet us. Harriet saw her and immediately reached out to her. I explained to Mrs. Prentice that we would try it a few days and come back to see how she was doing. That seemed agreeable to everyone.

A few days later, when we went back to check, Harriet was happy to see us, but seemed so content, we all agreed we had made a wise decision, and Harriet stayed. *Thank you Lord.*

Chapter 13

A Letter for Sarah
Mid-March 1829

    William and Sarah went to Mr. Cheney Taft's store today in Northbridge Center, and since Mr. Taft was also the postman, he told them there was a letter waiting for Sarah. She had never before received a letter in her life. In fact, I don't remember any of us receiving mail. It had been written weeks before, but we seldom go to the store, and since we attend Sabbath meeting in South Sutton, we had no occasion to see Mr. Taft before this. In his excitement, William forgot to buy half of what he went for.

    Sarah carefully opened the letter which was written by the cousin from Bristol County that she had met for the first time at Mother's funeral.

> "Dear Cousin Sarah,
>
> "I think of you often since meeting you at your mother's funeral last October. We seemed to become instant friends, and yet neither of us has made close friends in our own towns. I want to get to know you better. I asked Mother and Father if you may come visit us for awhile. They are willing and will send the money for you to take the stagecoach if your family gives permission. I think you would enjoy

seeing what it is like to live in a town, and since I only have one brother left at home, I would dearly love to have another girl in the house. I have wonderful plans for us. A singing school will be starting soon at the meeting house just down the road from us, and there are girls' anti-slavery societies and ever so many activities for young people in our town. You will be surprised to see how many other relatives share your last name and heritage. You have more relations than you have ever dreamed of.

"Please write me soon to tell me your answer. I hope you will be able to stay at least a few months. Mother says you were named after her."

Your "new" cousin,
Prudence Williams

William and Sarah hurried to Aunt Elizabeth's house in Northbridge since she was Father's sister and would know the relatives on that side of the family. Aunt Elizabeth assured Sarah that she would indeed have a marvelous time and that Aunt Sarah, who was hers and Father's sister, and Uncle Timothy were fine Christian parents and had a delightful sense of humor. Aunt Elizabeth thought it was a wonderful idea for the poor darling.

Sarah came home and showed us the letter with a look of total bewilderment on her face. She is the last person we would have expected to receive a special invitation to pay an extended visit with a distant relative. She who is so quiet and off in her own world.

"It would mean the loss of some income because you would not be sewing shoe uppers any more, and I would no longer have your help on laundry and baking days," I said thinking out loud. "You would no longer be there to read aloud to William and me while we worked or talk William out of his melancholy moods."

At first, it seemed that there was no question she should go, but now I realized for the first time how dependent I had become on her. William's excitement had also worn off as he realized the implications. What seemed at first like an innocent invitation now seemed like a menacing threat to destroy our family. William walked outside and began currying his oxen, and I began kneading my bread far harder than I had before.

As if the news were not enough to totally unsettle us, just then an oxcart passed down the road. It was heaped high with all the earthly belongings of one of our neighbors who was leaving soon for the Northwest. So many Sutton residents had been moving there since Gen. Putnam, from Sutton, started settling Ohio a number of years ago. I looked out the window and saw William watching it go by. He stood gazing down the road long after it was out of sight.

Sarah went into the parlor to be alone. Thankfully, the younger children were still in school. Otherwise, quiet thought would have been an impossibility.

As I continued to knead my bread, I remembered that I had been planning to suggest singing school to Sarah myself.

"Sarah," I called out to her. "Please come help me with baking so we can talk and work at the same time." We began shaping the bread dough into rolls together. "I know it will seem as if I am competing with your cousin, but we have a singing school starting up soon in our meeting house, too. I was planning to suggest that you attend because I noticed your lovely voice when you were singing the children to sleep one night. You must have inherited it from Mother. Do you remember when she used to sing around the house before Father died?"

"Yes, of course I do, though I expect the younger children probably wouldn't remember. The singing school does interest me."

"I guess I feel a little like Mother did when Nancy got her teaching job," I said. "I didn't expect this, and it has taken me quite by surprise. Part of me wants to encourage you to go and get new experiences and make new friends, and part of me realizes how much I depend on you, and how much I want our family to stay together. I know it sounds exciting to meet the rest of the relatives especially when you liked this one cousin so much. What do you think about it?"

"At first, I was so excited, I just laughed and laughed, and now," she hesitated and her chin began to quiver, "it seems so complicated. I just wish Mother were still alive and that I could just leave and have a good time." She stopped to cry quietly and blow her nose. "It wouldn't be fair for me to leave if it meant the family would suffer. A few months ago, I wasn't that important to the family, and now it seems like if I go, the whole family could fall apart. How could that be?"

"I wish Nancy were here," I said. "She would know what to do,"

Sarah's eyes brightened and she said, "That's it. Nancy will be coming home unless she decides to teach for summer term. Then you won't need me around the house so much."

"If she doesn't teach, we won't have her income, though," I reminded her.

"What if I just went for one month, and I took a supply of shoe uppers with me to work on while I was there? I could go in a few weeks when winter term is over and Mariah and Abigail will be home to help around the house and take care of Harriet if she comes back. Miranda would take care of Lucretia. That way the family income would be the same and I could still see what it's like to live in another town and get to know our relatives. Maybe Prudence could help me sew the uppers," she said.

"I think you have come up with a very good solution. Talk to William and see if he sees any problems with it," I said.

Sarah skipped out the door, happier than I ever remembered seeing her. She grabbed onto William and jumped and danced around as she told him her plan. I watched from the kitchen window. William smiled and gave a nod of his head which sent her flying through the barnyard to tell all the chickens, cows and oxen the good news. I thought we would need to get a rope to tie her down to earth.

Chapter 14

Our Family Upset
April 1829

We made a family event out of seeing Sarah off. We put her bags and a supply of shoe uppers into the oxcart, and she and William sat on the cart. We even got Harriet from Mrs. Prentice's for the occasion. Sarah held Harriet closely on her lap and talked to her constantly the whole way to the county road and up to the Cheney Taft's store where the stagecoach came to pick her up. The rest of us walked beside the cart. We had made arrangements for her to stay overnight in Providence at the home of the family of Rebecca Bradford, with whom Nancy teaches, and she was to arrive at Cousin Prudence's house in Rehoboth the next day. She looked so pretty in the spick-and-span new lavender dress we had all sewn for her. That, too, was a family project and even Lucretia helped with the hem.

The first letter we received from her caused plenty of excitement.

"Dear Family,

"I arrived at Cousin Prudence's house the day after I left, but not without incident. Riding in a stagecoach is like being inside a butter churn. I am glad my teeth were firmly rooted in my mouth or they might all have fallen out. The other passengers were pleasant enough, but we were packed in so tightly that it was rather too close for conversation. We seemed to politely ignore one another mainly, except for occasional short comments regarding bumps in the road. I felt like applesauce by the time I reached Providence. My accommodations there with the Bradfords were very comfortable and doubly so since it meant I could be out of the butter churn for several hours. The next day, I entered into the stagecoach with much less enthusiasm than I had the day before, knowing what awaited me.

"About half-way to Rehoboth, a wheel fell off and the stagecoach nearly overturned. We stopped abruptly and passengers disembarked. While waiting for the wheel to be fixed, a torrential rain storm began which left us all thoroughly soaked as rats, our hair hanging in ringlets around our eyes, and shivering with cold. This turn of events caused the gentleman riding with me to smoke even more heavily than before. My dress soaked up the smoke so that by the time I reached our dear relatives, I smelled like a manufactory, was sopping wet and was coughing and sneezing. This caused them to pamper and pet me even more than I think they would have, and I quickly felt a part of the family.

"Aunt Sarah is so kind and loves to bake little sweetmeats for us, like peppermint drops or ginger nuts. It feels so good to have a mother again. Uncle Timothy loves to tease, has a hearty laugh and is fond of jokes—yet is steady as a clock. Yesterday, after seeing the shoe uppers I had brought, he asked me, 'What shoemaker makes shoes without using leather, but uses the four elements of air, fire, water and earth?' The answer is a blacksmith. Uncle Timothy seems to be glad to have someone around who hasn't heard his jokes yet. He laughs at his own jokes much harder than anyone else and we end up laughing at him.

"The boy cousin, Isaac, who is William's age, has kept his distance and just watches me quietly. I suppose, in time, we will become friendly. He has been working on a small model of a hot air balloon and occasionally tries to send it up. Something always goes wrong, however, and the whole thing has gone up in flames more than once. Sometimes in the evenings, Uncle Timothy teaches him how to play the violin. Uncle Timothy plays quite well and sometimes accompanies the hymn-singing at meeting. Cousin Isaac's playing is still somewhat squeaky.

"I do miss you all so much. Only having five in a family seems so little. I miss the commotion of you all at the dinner table. I miss Lucretia telling us what she learned in school and I miss holding Harriet, and the little girlish behavior of Miranda, Mariah and Abigail, and Betsey and Nancy's big-sister advice and William's quiet ways and the oxen and big brother Jonathan and the chickens and the farm. I admit I do not miss the pigs.

"Girls here spend so much more time prinking* and looking just right, and my best lavender dress seems so plain. Prudence has let me borrow her extra dresses so I won't feel so out of place.

"I went to Singing School once so far because it meets just once per week. The singing master lives in another town, and the town of Rehoboth hires him to come just one night. At first the other girls seemed strange to me, but by the end of the evening I had become a friend with a couple of them. We sang some Scottish melodies as well as hymn tunes. I liked it very much.

"Every week, there is a new speaker or painter or entertainer of some kind at the Lyceum. We watched a theorem painter last night. He painted the scene of Daniel in the Lion's Den. Next week, there will be a phrenologist who claims he can determine what kind of person you are by feeling the bumps on your head. I may not get to hear that one. It's too strange, yet people believe it sincerely.

"I have not begun working on shoe uppers but I know my obligation and plan to begin by next week. I am already feeling so much at home here and our farm and way of life seem so distant.

"I wish all of you could come here, too. I know now I will find it very difficult to leave at the end of the month. Please write to me and tell me what everyone is doing.

Affectionately,
Sarah

PS It's so strange to meet so many relatives who share our last name and some of our first names, too. There are Carpenters everywhere you turn. I am learning all about Father's father and grandfather and I've seen the farm where they lived. Our great-grandfather was an important man in town, but I will tell you all about that when I come home."

I finished reading the letter and began to wonder if life would ever be the same. I couldn't imagine Sarah being content to live on our farm again. Yet we were family.

Nancy finished winter term and came home the week after Sarah's letter arrived. She will be teaching summer term but has a break now. I showed her the letter and watched her reactions as she read. Nancy pursed her lips and looked up at me with a sigh, then folded her hands together and made a church steeple out of her index fingers and began tapping the steeple against her lips. She was silent for a long time and just looked at the floor then finally said, "Things will never be the same."

Harriet had come back when school break began, and just then, she woke up from her nap. Nancy got her out of bed. She is two years old now and growing out of her baby ways. When she first wakes up, though, she likes to be held for awhile. She is full of mischief and began pulling Nancy's hair out of her bonnet. Nancy finally took the bonnet off. Harriet looked at the two of us and said, "Mama." Nancy asked if she called me that. She doesn't. It is just seemingly a word without meaning that she says occasionally. I wondered if she called Mrs. Prentice "Mama."

"Betsey, who is her mother now?" Nancy asked. "We all share the responsibility of her care now, but what is to become of her in the future? If you get married in a few years, will you take her with you? Then what about the others? Where will they go? What if Sarah doesn't want to stay with us any more? Will any young man even be interested in us if he knows he must become a father to half-grown children right away? Is it fair or even possible to find a young man in a position to support a young family?"

"I was hoping to ask you those questions," I said. "I don't have any answers. I just have more questions. Is it right to keep Jonathan in a position of keeping the family together and making it impossible for him to begin saving to start a family of his own? Is it right to try to make William stay when he wants to get away and make a new start? What should we do?"

Nancy answered, "I don't know if we should keep on as we are as much as we can and just make changes as we need to, or if we should make plans to find other homes for some of us. I think the ones of us that signed the agreement need to get together and talk again."

Harriet got down and Nancy tied a rope around her then tied the other end to a table leg so she couldn't get near the fire. She played contentedly for awhile, and when she began to fuss, Lucretia came to take her to another room to play.

"Lucretia, come here. Let me have a look at you before you run off with baby Harriet. How many teeth have you lost now?" Nancy asked.

"Four. Thee my two big teeth coming in on the bottom? Two more are looth," Lucretia said.

"You look like an old grandma right now, you funny little girl. Run along and play with the baby now."

Harriet came over and stomped her feet. "I not baby. I, Haywiet."

"Oh, you are, are you? All right, Haywiet, it is," Nancy said and gave her a big hug.

Jonathan came home on Saturday afternoon after his half-day at the mill, and the four of us older ones got together after our nooning. Harriet was taking a nap, and the other girls were playing outside.

Jonathan, Nancy, William and I sat down at the table and looked at one another for awhile, not knowing how to proceed. Jonathan began by saying, "I have had a lot of time to think while working in the mill. It's so noisy, you can't talk to anyone, and the days are so long and hot and boring. First of all, I can tell you I don't want to spend my life working twelve-hour days in a hot, noisy mill. At the end of a day, I begin to feel like a machine myself. I'm ready to feel like a human being again. I have been regretting that I didn't learn Father's plough-making trade, and I would like to see if Uncle Ellis would be interested in letting me be an apprentice in his plough shop in Douglas. It shouldn't take long since I do remember some things from Father. Uncle Ellis would surely allow me to take time off when I need to come home and farm, too."

Nancy then spoke up. "I feel very much like a human being as a teacher. Sometimes I feel too human and would like to strangle a few so-called scholars, but most of the time I like it, and I like living in different families' homes. You certainly get to see another side of the students when you live with them. Sometimes, a well-behaved scholar will be a monster in his own home. Other times, a mischievous scholar will be angelic at home. It makes me realize why parents are sometimes surprised when I tell them what their child is like in the schoolhouse. I could go on and on, but the main point now is that I think I would be happy teaching, if the Lord wills, for several more years."

William shifted uncomfortably in his chair and just kept staring down, so I decided to take my turn to speak. "I am content to continue doing what I am doing, working at home and taking care of the children for now. I dream of marrying some day but wonder if I have any right to hope for such a thing when my sisters will continue to need me for years to come." I stopped and just held my head in my hands.

William cleared his throat and took a deep breath and hesitated, and finally stammered, "I-I-I know we hafta think of more than ourselves. I love our family, too; but is staying together really the most important thing? Why do we think that?" He looked around sheepishly, his eyes not really meeting any of ours. He stood up and walked anxiously around, then continued. "I want to go out West to Ohio or Illinois. There's not enough land here for all of us anyway. And as for the family staying together, maybe it wouldn't be so bad if the little girls were in families with a mother and father. Some of the relatives would be happy to have them just as Uncle Timothy and Aunt Sarah are happy to have Sarah."

Miranda happened to walk in the door at this time and stared in disbelief. "Miranda, you go back outside and play. We are just talking," I said.

Miranda burst into tears and came running over to me hug me. "I don't care if I don't have a mother and father. Don't send me away." She ran to William and cried, "William, don't go," and turned and ran to her room where we could hear her sobbing.

William found it even harder to speak now, but he continued. "I might seem hard-hearted, but I'm not gonna change my mind just 'cause she's crying."

Nancy replied, "We can't just ignore her, either, William. We have to remember that decisions we make affect other people. The children are your sisters, after all."

I wanted to run from the room and cry myself, but I knew that would just make things worse. No one knew what to say and there was awkward silence for some time.

Lucretia came running in. "Abigail and Mariah won't let me play with them and I don't know where Miranda is."

We looked at one another. It was only a matter of time before Miranda would tell the others why she was upset and what she heard. We needed more time.

"Lucretia, tell Abigail and Mariah about the new-born lambs down at Mr. Martin's place. I think they would like to go see them with you. Run along," I said. She got excited about that and ran outside again.

Jonathan said, "William is right about needing to make decisions that we have really thought about. If Miranda tells the others what she heard, we are going to have four crying girls on our hands who will make it impossible to think."

Nancy said, "We need to pray for God's help. One thing I have been learning from the preacher at the Methodist meeting this winter is that we try to solve problems by ourselves instead of asking God for help. We claim to be Christians but act like pagans. God is our Father and He wants us to ask Him for help. Even Miranda knows that. I'm going to have her come down here and pray with us."

Nancy brought a red-eyed, tear-stained Miranda back with her. Jonathan offered his handkerchief, and she made such a racket blowing her nose, we all had to laugh.

"Miranda, we want to do what is right for our family to make everyone the happiest, but we don't know what to do. We would like you to help us pray about it. Will you?" Nancy said.

She nodded her head, and said, "We should have Abigail and Mariah and Lucretia help us pray, too."

"We don't want to upset them like we did you," I said.

Nancy said we should start with the Lord's prayer and remember that the first thing Jesus prayed for was that God's will be done on earth as it is in heaven. She sounded like a preacher, but we needed to hear it. Our prayers were very awkward and short, but we all felt much better when we were done.

A knock came at the door, and we looked at one another, half expecting a miracle new mother and father to appear. Instead, it was Deacon Welcome Whipple.

"I was just passing by and decided to stop in and see how you young folks were doing," he said holding his hat in his hand, a perfect gentleman.

Nancy said, "I think God sent you. We are very confused right now."

"What has happened?" he asked.

We all looked at one another and had to think just what had happened. Nothing, in a sense. Yet everything in another sense. I explained all that we had talked about and said we were wondering what would happen to the family, and if we could ever expect to marry in the future when we have so many little ones dependent on us.

"I'm not little. I'm eight years old," Miranda said.

"I know you're very grown up, but I mean you can't live by yourself. You still need someone to care for you," I answered. "Miranda, look out the window. See Mrs. Nolen in her yard trying to work with little Horace tugging at her dress? Why don't you go help her. This is grown-up talk."

Miranda pouted and finally left as Jonathan gently helped her out the door. She called out behind her, "You better not give me away."

Deacon Whipple said, "I see the problem."

"You have a lot more to think about than most young people your age," he said. "I can see that you all love your family very much. That would please your parents if they could see it. But you are also struggling with individual goals, which is natural—William especially. Let me start with Jonathan in my advice-giving. I know your Uncle Ellis and I know of his plough-making business in Douglas. Before I moved here to Sutton a few years back to take care of my aging parents, I used to live in Douglas and I owned a cotton mill. Your Uncle Ellis is a fine, hard-working man, but he is not very forward-looking. He is still making the old-fashioned wooden ploughs, which were fine in their day, but the new cast-iron ploughs being made in Worcester and Hingham and being shown at the county fairs are superior. He will be ruined if he doesn't keep pace with progress."

"If you go to learn the wood plough-making trade, you will be investing years of your life into a dead enterprise. Now, I know working at the Northbridge cotton mill is not the most pleasant of employments, and I agree that you should not plan to spend the rest of your life there. But for now, it gives you a cash income that your family needs, you can buy what you need at the company store, and you can learn from the experience if you apply yourself. I understand that the owner's son, John Whitin, is about your age and a very bright young man. He is working on various inventions. You would do well to befriend him and work with him if you can."

Jonathan looked discouraged and said, "I suppose you're right. I cannot abide working there too much longer, though. I will go deaf, and it means I can't live at home during the winter months, either. I have met John Whitin but I don't know how to go about getting to work with him; he has worked in the mill off and on since he was nine years old."

"I know his father, Paul Whitin, quite well, so I will put in a good word for you," Deacon Whipple said. "Your family survived without you this winter. It is good that you move back home in the warmer months so you can help William keep the farm running, though. Thank goodness we don't run the mills like they do up north of here. For them, the mill is their life, and they wouldn't be able to farm if they worked in the mill. In fact, single girls there do most of the mill work up.

"Now, for Betsey. You must be nearly twenty-one now if I remember correctly."

"Next month," I replied.

"Well, I will see if I can get your father and mother's will probated as soon as possible, because as I recall, each of you will get some inheritance when you turn twenty-one. I helped your father write his will when he realized he was dying. Unfortunately, for some reason it takes years to get these wills probated. A poor person could die of starvation waiting. You mentioned marriage. If I may be so bold, are there any prospects on the horizon?"

"No, not really," I answered.

"Well, I want to warn you that word gets around when young ladies come into an inheritance, and there may be some prospects when the will is probated," he said.

"Thank you for your advice. I will remember that. On the other hand, having some money may make the difference between marrying or not if the person you really want to marry is quite poor," I added. Why did I need to say that?

"That is true. Just keep your head about you," he said. "Now Nancy is in a comfortable position for the time being, aren't you? You are making a steady income at employment that you enjoy and at your age, I hope you are not thinking of marriage."

"Only the idea of marriage, Deacon Whipple. I think we need to think how marriage will affect the younger ones. If one of us married and moved away, should we feel obligated to take some of the children with us, and if so, which ones?"

"Don't worry about tomorrow. Sufficient to the day are the evils thereof," he replied. "We can spend time making elaborate plans about tomorrow, and when tomorrow comes, the circumstances may be so different from what we anticipated, our decisions don't apply. You told me you prayed together and started out with 'Thy kingdom come, thy will be done.' If each of you keeps that in mind as you make each decision, God will work things out for you for the best. I need to remind you that the best isn't necessarily the easiest though. I would be happy to talk and pray with you more as decisions arise. You know, I used to be a member of the Society of Friends, or Quakers as others call us, and a part of me still is. We Friends aren't afraid to wait in silence for hours at a time until we are sure that God is speaking to us. These days, when people pray, they think they have to do all the talking. We need to learn to listen to God, too, though. The Bible says we should be slow to speak and fast to listen. That is good advice, and it refers to how to pray to God, as well.

"And now, William," he started, but at this point, Abigail came running inside.

"Jonathan and William, come quickly, one of the cows is trying to deliver a calf and is having trouble."

William and Jonathan ran out to the barn and Deacon Whipple joined them. The cow was lying there mooing loudly and was obviously in pain. Deacon Whipple called out, "She is trying to deliver the head first. Wash your hands quickly and come over here."

Both of them ran to the pump, quickly washed and ran back in.

"Let me see your hands. William, your hands are slightly smaller; come here and do as I say. Push the calf's head back in and reach in there and find its feet."

William said, "I can't; it's too tight."

"I know it's tight, but you've got to do it anyway. Be persistent. There you go. Can you feel the calf's hooves? Pull them out. Work as fast as you can, or the calf will suffocate."

William struggled and winced and pushed and pulled and finally the calf's hooves appeared. Immediately, a small gingerbread-colored calf was effortlessly delivered.

"Drag the calf over to its mother so she will lick the membrane off its face, and it can breathe," Deacon Whipple said.

William did so, and we all cheered and laughed as the mother licked her calf until it was quite clean. William looked pleased on the one hand but disgusted with what a mess he was.

"Thank you Deacon Whipple," he said "I'm sorry I can't shake your hand. Looks like we'll have another ox to train." He then quickly went out to the pump to get cleaned up.

Deacon Whipple said, "Well, that was exciting, I must say." He called out, "William, you did an excellent job. You are a natural at delivering calves." Then turning back to the rest of us, he said, "Whoever does the milking here, remember to only milk two of the teats; the calf will need some nourishment now."

"Thank you, Mr. Whipple, we are old hands at that," I said.

"Yes, yes, of course. I'm sounding like a mother hen. Well, I really must be going. It would be hopeless to try to continue our earlier conversation at this point. We will talk later. Good day to you all. And God bless you. My prayers are with you, and remember what I said about taking time to listen to God."

Chapter 15

My Twenty-first Birthday
May 1829

    I had looked forward to May, the month I became twenty-one and the month to begin planting the gardens and crops. The apple orchards were full of delicate pink blossoms; it was breath-taking. May is a time of new beginnings anyway, and this year I expected to feel somehow more independent. Instead, it began in a very disappointing way. One morning at the beginning of the month, I found a note on the table when I got up to make breakfast. It was from William.
    It read,

> "Dear Family,
>
> "By now I am on my way West with another family from town. I will write all about it later. Please do not try to find me or stop me. I love you, but I knew you would try to talk me out of it. I was hoping Sarah would come home before I left. I will miss her especially. I took a pair of Father's plough handles with me that was out in the barn. I am not running away. I am making a new start. Pray for me.
>
>   Love,
>   William

PS I kept the cash from the last batch of shoes that I bottomed. I will make it up to you, and last September, I didn't tell you that I shot a muskrat and kept the $5.00 reward. So I have plenty of money for awhile."

Jonathan read it and just shook his head and sighed. "I didn't think he would do it this way. I knew he would go sometime; he was set on it. Five dollars! That's a lot of money for him to keep secret all this time." He went outside and began chopping wood.

The week before, we had received a letter from Sarah asking if she could stay another month. William had seemed unusually sad. Now, we realized why. They had become close in the past few months. That must be why he insisted on adding a paragraph when we wrote her back.

We needed to write to her again to tell her to come home. We must have more help on the farm since William wouldn't be there to help with planting, and we needed more cash income. I found myself thinking that Sarah had no right to be content attending singing school and lectures and wearing fancy dresses while we all worked so hard on the farm. *Lord, forgive me.* I better wait until some of my bitterness goes away and I can write to her in a loving way. She will never want to come home if I write her in the mood I am in now.

I woke Nancy and showed her the letter from William. She surprised me by being very angry with William. "He's only thinking of himself. Why doesn't he consider how his leaving affects everyone else? Now we won't have the money from the shoe bottoms he made, and we will not have his help on the farm. Where does he get these big ideas? I guess there is nothing we can do about it now. I don't even know what family in town was moving out West, and we have no horse to pursue him anyway. He needs our prayers all right," she said, and began brushing her long hair vigorously. "Let's do laundry today, Betsey. I need to take my anger out by scrubbing clothes, or I will be snapping at the children all day. OOH! Now, we have to haul all the water in, since he's not here. It is all my fault for letting him know that girls could haul water, too, when he wanted to work on the canal last autumn."

Jonathan brought the wood to the porch then went out to the barn to lead the oxen out to pasture. He came running back to the house all excited. "The other cow delivered in the night. We have another healthy calf. Thank heaven."

Nancy and I went out to see the new little calf nursing vigorously from its mother. We patted the cow and assured her that she had done a good job and brought her some fresh hay and water. The new calf was the pretty gingerbread color of all the cows but had a few spots of white that looked like whipped cream. There is nothing like a new-born animal to brighten your day. *Thank you, God; you knew we needed that just now.*

I saw Olive Nolen out in her yard and told her the news of William. She shook her head and said, "Maybe it's better this way. He wasn't happy here and you know he dreaded all the ploughing he was going to have to do very soon. Doesn't he realize there will be ploughing out West, too? I don't know. I don't know. I'm surprised the other family he went with didn't insist on permission from someone. He is only fifteen. I wonder if he really went with another family or if he just went by himself and figured he would meet up with other families. I will tell Mr. Nolen about it and see what he says. Maybe he will want to hire Mr. Burden to ride his horse and try to find him." She went inside while I waited outside.

She returned after a few minutes and shook her head. "Mr. Nolen said to just let him be. Some young men just have it in their blood I guess. Maybe after a few years he will come back and live on his land and be perfectly content. You just never know."

I pictured him coming back in a few years. Where would we be? Maybe he would be like the man in "The Legend of Sleepy Hollow" that Sarah read to us. He came back and found his children had grown and everything was different. Suddenly, I began to cry and Olive put her arms around me. "I've been so surprised and angry at him. Now, I just realized I may never see him again. Who knows what could happen to him or us in the coming years when you see what has happened to us in the last two or three." I went running for home and just got to the necessary in time to be really sick. Olive followed me and put her hand on my back to comfort me.

"William, oh William, why did you have to do this?" I said.

Olive went in our house, got me a cool cloth to wash with and asked Nancy to make me some tea. "I would stay and do it myself if I didn't have to worry about what mischief Horace has gotten into. Mr. Nolen just does not watch him carefully. I will check on you later. I'm so sorry." She hurried out the door.

Mariah and Abigail came wandering in followed by Miranda, and we had to explain what happened. Soon, all of us were sitting around the table crying. Miranda had a crazy notion that somehow she had made him go because she had yelled at him, so we had to assure her that that had nothing to do with it. Lucretia and Harriet were awakened by all the commotion. Lucretia was heart-broken, too, but seemed more sad at seeing us crying and went around comforting us all. Harriet, of course, was too young to understand and just thought William had gone "Bye, Bye." She did make a brief attempt to cry with us, and offered to give each one of us her favorite blanket, which was so cute, it made us all laugh instead. Our combination of laughing, crying and nose blowing made us quite a sight for nearly an hour. We then had enough of it, and proceeded to get dressed and make breakfast and clean up, all the time comforting each other and sniffling for another couple of hours.

Nobody ate much for breakfast, nor did we feel like a big nooning, so the whole day was spent in a sort of partial existence, the bright spot being the new calf. Never was there a calf so welcome as that one. We probably would have called it "Welcome" if that had not been our dear friend Deacon Whipple's first name.

We ended the day by writing a letter to Sarah, telling her that William had gone and asking her to please come home. For awhile, we thought maybe we should try to get along without her, but then we realized how much we wanted her to be a part of the family again and that she would probably want to come home when she heard about William. It was almost like having another funeral. It was a time that you felt the whole family needed to be there to share the sadness.

Lucretia even insisted on writing a little all by herself. She wrote,

"Der Sara, I mis yu so mutch. Wen ar yu cummin hom? I rot dis bi misef. I los anover toof. Luv, LUCRETIA." Then she drew a picture of the new calf, complete with spots. It looked more like a frog, but she labeled it "caf" to make it perfectly clear.

A week later, Sarah returned, and it felt so good to have her back. She looked different at first. Her hair and dress were fancy, but within two days, she was one of us again and happy to be home. We eagerly listened to her tell us all about life in Rehoboth and all of our relatives. She told it so well. I was sure we would all ask her to tell it all again. Of course, she hoped to go visit them again. She seems so grown up. In six weeks' time, she has aged two years. It made me ashamed that I had been angry with her once for going.

She put on an old dress and went out to curry William's oxen. She talked to them the whole time, consoling them on their loss of William, and telling them all about Rehoboth. They listened contentedly, swishing the flies off with their tails and blinking lazily, chewing their cud.

She washed up out in the yard and came in the house. "I warned the 'boys' that ploughing season was here, and that they had their work cut out for them. Tomorrow, Jonathan, I think we better put their yokes on so we can remind them how that feels. I also need to remind them a little of the routine of walking together, and then the next day I will help you a little with ploughing, if you want. We need to break them in easy. They have lost a lot of weight over the winter. I didn't think I would want to help on the farm again after tasting the town life, but it feels so good to walk around in bare feet, feeling the dirt and handling the animals. I didn't know I missed it. I think I'll start training that calf that William delivered."

Jonathan smiled. "My, you have gotten to be bossy in six weeks time. You know exactly what you want and when and where." He gave her a hug.

I had to smile. Maybe we should see about sending the other girls away for awhile. Abigail was almost twelve and a half. I think I will ask Aunt Elizabeth for names of relatives with children her age. Though, Mariah would be lost without her. Maybe I should find someone who would take them both!

For my twenty-first birthday, I was not allowed to do any work, and the children brought me wildflowers and breakfast in bed. They made a wonderful nooning, too. Nancy, of course, did most of the cooking, including a birthday cake. Jonathan bought me a tortoise shell comb at the company store, and Nancy bought me a beautiful new bonnet. I felt like a queen. Nancy helped me wash my hair. It felt so good to be clean again for the first time in months. Olive and Mr. Nolen bought me a copy of Mrs. Child's *The American Frugal Housewife*. *Lord, help me to be grateful even though I don't like to be reminded I am a housewife with no husband.*

One warm day, Nancy and I walked to the Rawson Tavern in Uxbridge where I still had some credit from when I made pantaloons for the Irish. I took along my new bonnet and chose some beautiful imported fabric to match it. I find myself using lavender colors of late since they bring back memories of Mother as I remembered her last Independence Day when she had looked so pretty. The fabric had come up on a canal boat from the port at Providence. Nancy and I made a new dress for me, and Sarah gave advice based on styles she had seen in Rehoboth. I felt like such an old woman getting advice on style from someone younger. I think I will wear this dress on Independence Day this year.

I told Nancy about my walk down to the canal with William last year and his teasing me about wanting to go for a ride on the canal boat.

Nancy said, "You should work hard this summer baking some of your delicious tarts and sewing collars and such. You could save enough to go on a canal boat by the end of summer. You could go up to Worcester, or better yet, go south on the canal to the port in Providence, Rhode Island." Her eyes lit up as she grabbed my hands and made me promise to do it.

"I wouldn't want to go alone, you silly goose. You come, too," I said. "We could go when you have finished teaching summer term, as a celebration. You will be eighteen by then. I will wear my new lavender dress and the bonnet you got me for my twenty-first birthday. I am so glad you thought of it."

Having something to look forward to would make the hot summer months more bearable. We set aside a little tin box to collect our coins in for the trip. *Oh, please God, don't let anything happen to spoil this.*

Chapter 16

A Visit from Cyrus
June 1829

Sarah was like a new person. We had been so afraid she wouldn't want to live on the farm any more and yet she threw herself into the ploughing and farm chores. She confided in me one day, "Since William left, I feel that I have to take his place and even do the ploughing that he dreaded. I think of him all the time and wonder what he is doing and where he is and if he is healthy...and if he will come back. I miss him terribly. I hope he really is with a family and not on his own somewhere. And, I hope he writes."

William had been like a cloud hanging over the house ever since Father had died. We hadn't realized how much we were used to the presence of that cloud. We were all different since he left—not necessarily better—but different. Any one person gone just changes things. That's all.

Seeing Sarah so diligent made me all the more determined to try to make Abigail and Mariah more helpful. Now that Abigail had mastered milking, I decided to teach her to make cheese. There was no reason for a girl her age to go to school during the summer when she could be helping around the house. So, I called her in one morning for her first lesson.

"Abigail, I want you to stay home from school this summer term and learn to do some things in the kitchen," I said. "Today I'm going to show you how we make cheese."

"I've watched you lots of times, and I am not interested. Besides, I was planning to improve my penmanship in school this summer. The school master this summer is supposed to have a very nice hand," she replied.

"I know you like learning to make all those fancy letters, but they are not going to put food on the table. You will most likely not marry a rich man who can just buy all the cheese you want while you sit around writing fancy letters in your fancy dress," I replied. "You are at a very good age to learn to make cheese, and watching someone else do it and doing it yourself are two different things."

"There you go again making plans for me instead of seeing what I want to do," she said and ran to her room crying.

Not again. What happened to that care-free, pleasant Abigail from last summer? I wished Mother were here to tell me how to deal with her. Who did Abigail think she was anyway thinking she could do as she pleased? Why should I be the only one with obligations to the family? It would be useless to make her watch me, so I left her alone and started making the cheese by myself, as usual, muttering the whole time. Abigail finally came out of her room but she avoided me and didn't speak to me at nooning. She washed the dishes with Mariah afterwards and I could hear her complaining softly to Mariah about me not caring about what she wanted.

I resisted the temptation to slap her and instead put Harriet down for a nap, took off my apron and went to Olive's house. She was resting in the shade of an oak tree, doing some of her fine needlework. I joined her and told her of Abigail's rebellion.

"I think I'll tell her she can't eat any more cheese if she won't help make it," I said.

"That may work," Olive said, "but it will cause bitterness. Why don't you suggest that if they make more cheeses than your family needs, you could sell some of the extra and let Abigail have some of the profit on the extras. You could start by having her write down the recipe in her best hand."

"Olive, you are a genius. You are so much like Nancy. Nancy would have thought of something like that, too. That's why she never needs to thrash the scholars when she teaches. I thank you for your advice. I hope it works." I went back home to drain the whey off and finish with the cheeses.

To my surprise, Jonathan and Cyrus were in the kitchen. I began blushing as usual, and Cyrus looked at me and raised his eyebrows, obviously pleased.

"Good afternoon, Miss Betsey," he said.

"Hello, Cyrus. Why aren't you two at the mill this afternoon?" I asked.

"So many of the workers had been excused to work on their farms, Mr. Whitin decided to only work the rest of us half day. He said the water was very low in the mill pond anyway. I knew there was plenty of work to be done here, so I brought Cyrus along to help," Jonathan answered.

"It's difficult for an outdoorsy man like me to tolerate the mill work anyway," Cyrus said in his charming Irish accent, "so your brother was so kind to invite me home. I look forward to working in the fresh air."

His accent made me smile and blush all the more. "Have you eaten yet?" I asked. I found myself imitating his accent without meaning to and we all laughed about that.

"Yes, we have," Jonathan answered. "John Whitin invited us home for nooning. That was quite an experience. They live in a very nice big home and have a special room just for eating; there are no beds in it! The odd thing was that they ate with their forks and only used knives for cutting. Naturally, I picked up my knife to eat with as usual but after looking around at everyone else, decided that I would try to eat with a fork. It was most unnatural. At first I was afraid I would poke my mouth with the tines, but I got used to it after awhile. They put it in their mouth with the tines horizontal. They were very good-natured about it.

"After eating, John showed us around the house. They have one of those new stoves in their kitchen. Mrs. Whitin said it was hard to get used to regulating the temperature in it since you cannot see the fire, and at first she was ready to throw it out. Now, she would never go back to cooking in the fireplace and in fact has covered over the fireplace opening. She said she never realized just how back breaking it was to lean over the coals all the time and now doesn't know how she did it for so many years.

"I saw a pile of old newspapers in the parlor and asked if I might take one home." Jonathan handed me one on our way out the door. I thought you would enjoy reading the news. It's the *Massachusetts Spy* from Worcester," he said.

"Oh thank you. I don't think we have had a newspaper in the house since Father died. It will be fun to see what is going on in the world," I said. I spread it out on the table, and my eyes flew quickly across the columns to one advertisement and short article after another. "It says a Benjamin Jacobs has just received 1,500 dozen artificial flowers to sell, oh and somebody else is selling those leghorn bonnets. I wonder how a straw bonnet ever got a name like that."

Jonathan looked over my shoulder and read, "There is a new mail arrangement between Worcester and Providence. The stagecoach will be coming through Sutton on Mondays, Wednesdays and Fridays. You can ride on it for ONLY $2.25."

"Can you imagine!" I exclaimed. "I thought it was bad to pay 50 cents to go that far on the canal. Oh, here is another article saying Great Britain 'will not remain a silent spectator' while Russia tries to conquer Turkey."

"Listen to this," Jonathan called out, "Someone in Worcester raised the frame of a house without the use of ardent spirits, and 'it is said to be the first instance of the kind in the town.'"

Cyrus came over and pointed to the article about some pirates from Cuba.

"Oh, isn't the world an interesting place! Jonathan, I shall need to put this paper away immediately, or I will end up wasting the whole afternoon reading it. I don't know how anyone finds the time to write up so many pages of news each week. And can you imagine setting the type to print six or eight pages every week? Tell me what else happened in the Whitin's household?"

"Mrs. Whitin is very involved in the Temperance Movement, so a lot of our conversation had to do with an upcoming meeting. Mr. Whitin also agrees with it, of course, and he likes for her to be involved in such things," Jonathan said. "She talked on and on about how people are given to drink so much these days. She is happy that Northbridge has agreed not to sell ardent spirits except for medicinal purposes. Of course, some are known to sell it on the sly."

"I don't approve of drunkenness, either," Cyrus said. "But these temperance people really want to totally abolish any ardent spirits, as they call 'em, not just do away with drunkenness. I just know that when we were buildin' the canal, we appreciated our jiggers of rum. It soothed the muscles and made the day seem not nearly so hot, though I admit that many a man drank far more than a jigger at night."

"Well, enough of this idle chit chat," Jonathan said. "Cyrus and I are going to sow some corn now that there is no danger of frost. Maybe we can get Sarah to help, too."

"I think Sarah is already busy with the strawberries. She is out in the garden on her hands and knees spreading out the new young plants. I can hardly wait for them to ripen," I said. "Maybe you can get Abigail to help if you can figure out how to ask in the right way so she doesn't bite your head off. Mariah, Miranda and Lucretia went to school today. I'm going to finish making the cheese, then do a little mending. I noticed you had some frayed collars that needed turning and some socks that needed some new feet knitted for them."

"Do you have any switchel made up?" Jonathan asked. "I'd like to take some with us to the field."

"Yes, there's some in the kitchen in a jug. Under the table, I think. I had to move everything for my cheeses. I made it as you like it, with a little less vinegar and more molasses than the way Father drank it. Would you mind taking the whey outside and dumping it in the pig trough on your way out?" I asked.

"Let me get that, Betsey," Cyrus said. "It reminds me of home. We always had hogs as well. Sometime, I'll tell ya of my home in Ireland."

"I would like that very much, and I'm sure the children would enjoy hearing of it at tea time," I said. Suddenly I felt like an old mother instead of a young woman.

As soon as they left, I milled the cheese, added the salt, drained it well and pressed it in the hoops. Then I ran about the house straightening up. I picked some wildflowers outside and then began choosing the nicest things we had from the pantry to get ready for tea time. The socks and collars would keep.

I heard Harriet waking from her nap and went to fetch her before she got fussy. I sat and held her for awhile and noticed she seemed warm—almost hot.

"Wanna drink," she said in a croaky voice. I took her with me to the kitchen so I could see her in better light. She had the beginnings of little spots on her face and neck. Oh, no. Why did every good day have to be ruined with something disagreeable?

I went to the door and called to Jonathan, but he was too far away to hear. Sarah was nearer by in the strawberry beds, so I caught her attention. "Sarah, don't come in the house, and tell everyone to stay out. Harriet has measles or smallpox or something, and I don't want anyone else exposed. We will have to be quarantined. Have Jonathan go for a doctor. I am not making the mistake of waiting too long. We need to find out if the rest of us are already contagious." Why couldn't you get sick on some other day, I said to myself. I was looking forward to a nice tea time with Cyrus.

Abigail came into the room. I had forgotten about her. I showed her the spots on Harriet's face and neck. She was starting to have swollen areas on her neck as well and cried when I touched them.

Abigail said, "Come here, Harriet, you poor thing. Abigail will hold you and rock you awhile."

"Thank you, Abigail," I said. "And, Abby, I'm sorry I upset you about making cheese. I would like for you to improve your penmanship, too. You and Mariah are going to need to stay home for awhile anyway, I fear, because of Harriet. For the next few days, at least, I would like you to help me, so we can make some extra money. Would you mind using your beautiful penmanship to write down the instructions? Then, you and Mariah will be able to make it occasionally on your own when I am busy with other things. And, if we make more than we need, we can trade it at the store for something special."

"I suppose not," she answered begrudgingly. She got up and took Harriet to the kitchen to get a cool cloth for her forehead.

Jonathan called in from the front door. "Dr. Robinson said there's nothing much he can do for Harriet. Just keep her comfortable. He said nobody gets smallpox these days. It has to be measles or chicken pox. She will feel better in a few days. If it's chicken pox, the red spots will turn to blisters and scab over. The rest of you may come down with it in a couple of weeks. Don't go out in public and don't have anybody else in who hasn't had them yet. I already had them, but Cyrus hasn't, so he is going back to town after he helps me sow the seed; I think I will go with him to keep him company. While I was up talking to Dr. Robinson, I stopped in at Mr. Taft's store to see if we had any mail, and look what just came in. I guess there's no reason why I need to stay outside, is there," he said as he came in to the kitchen and handed us the letter.

"A letter from William! Go get Sarah," I said.

It was written in small letters on the back of an advertisement. He had made an envelope for it out of another scrap of paper.

> "Dear Family,
>
> "Don't worry about me. I am well. I walked and hitched rides with folks heading west in covered wagons through Connecticut and New York. People took pity on me when I told them I had no parents. I helped them in exchange for a ride and some meals. I went by ferry across the Hudson River to New Jersey. You would be surprised how many people there are 'westering.' There's covered wagons, people on a horse with a pack, folks with wheelbarrows, and a few like me walking with a pack on their backs. When I get to Pittsburgh, I'll try to get a ride on a flatboat down the Ohio River. I hear many people build their own, so if I help, I figure I'll be allowed passage.
>
> "I am in good health, and I hope you are, too. I pray for you every day and miss you very much. I must confess I lied to you about leaving with a family from town. I went by myself, but I didn't want you to worry.
>
> "I hope to be writing the next letter from Ohio. I miss you. I guess I said that already."
>
> Love,
> William

I had to have Jonathan read it. I cried the whole time, and Sarah joined me for a good cry at the end. We were relieved, happy, sad, and mad all at the same time.

Abigail said, "I ought to go to Ohio, too."

I replied, "You surely would have no time for penmanship if you did. If you think it is terrible to make cheese, imagine what it would be like not to have a home, and to live on a covered wagon or flatboat, and not have water and a kitchen nearby."

"It would be hard work, but it would be an adventure," she answered.

"You get any such notion out of your head. You are too young and a girl besides. There is plenty of adventure here on our farm."

Jonathan came over and said, "Let's see some of that penmanship I've been hearing about. Write down something nice, like a poem for me."

"I don't know a poem by heart," she said.

"Then write a hymn or a verse from the Bible," he said, retrieving the Bible from the little side table across the room.

He opened it and flipped through the pages awhile looking for something appropriate, and settled on Romans 8:38 and 39. "Write these verses. They're the ones you are supposed to be memorizing for Sunday School anyway."

She very carefully, in her best hand, wrote for him:

"For I am persuaded that neither death, nor life, nor angels, nor principalities, nor powers, nor things present, nor things to come, nor height, nor depth, nor any other creature, shall separate us from the love of God, which is in Christ Jesus our Lord."

"Beautiful!" he exclaimed. "What it says and how it is written are both beautiful. I will make a frame for it some day. Keep it in a safe place until I do."

"Show Cyrus," Abigail said.

"Great idea. I almost forgot about him working out there by himself. You carry it out; my hands are too dirty," Jonathan said.

A few minutes later, we could hear Cyrus exclaiming, "That is beautiful, me lass. You did that yourself, did you? You are quite an artist." She came back in the house beaming.

Sarah took care of Harriet while Abigail and I packed up some cold meat, cheese, bread and lemonade for Cyrus and Jonathan. They had their tea time outside so Cyrus would not be exposed to Harriet. Abigail and I sat and visited awhile with them, Abigail obviously delighted to be in the presence of people who admired her penmanship so much.

We asked Cyrus to tell us about Ireland. He suddenly turned serious and said wistfully, "O Ireland is a pretty land. Tis very green with rolling hills because it rains so much. I lived in a wee little house made of mud with a thatch roof, but we do not own our land and houses as you do. Most of our crops go to the English land owners who work us to death and barely leave us anythin' to eat. If we complain, they come tip over our houses or set them on fire and tell us to get out. Tis a sorry life. Most of us are Catholic, and the British hate us for that as well."

Abigail looked solemn but then brightened. "You must be glad to be in America. It's so different here. We get to own our land."

"Well, you do, that is for sure, but folks is not too anxious to give the Irish a helpin' hand here, neither. Tis very hard for the Irish to find a job, and when they do, it pays poorly. And no one seems to want to have an Irishman for a neighbor, though they were happy to have us build their canals. I saved some money from my work on the canal, but it seems that when I want to buy some land, it suddenly is not for sale. They won't even let the dead Irish be buried in their cemeteries. The bodies are taken to Rhode Island for burial."

"That's terrible," I said.

"Maybe we could sell you some of our land," Abigail answered brightly.

Jonathan answered, "That would be nice Abigail, but when our land gets divided up between ten children, there will not be much for any one of us."

"I would still sell you some of my land," she answered.

"That is so kind of you to say that, miss, but by the time you are twenty-one and can sell it, I will have moved away from here," he answered.

"Well, then why don't you marry Betsey," she said.

I covered my face with my apron. "Abigail, how could you?" I ran to the house. Children! How could she say such a thing?

Jonathan and Cyrus just laughed till their sides ached, and Abigail thought she had been so clever. When she came in the house later, I scolded her.

"Abigail, how could you say such a thing? First of all, it is not up to you to propose marriage for someone else, and second of all, you don't marry someone just so you can own some land. You embarrassed me terribly. I don't think I shall be able to look at Cyrus again."

"Well, I don't see why it is so bad. You are probably both thinking it anyway," she answered.

Sarah asked what had happened, and when I told her, she understood how embarrassing it was for me.

Jonathan and Cyrus soon left to go back to town, and Cyrus called into the house, "Thank you lassies for a won-n-nderful tea time." As they got further down the road, we could hear them laughing again.

Abigail shouted out the door, "Come again, Cyrus."

Lucretia took care of Harriet. She "peetended" Harriet was a baby bird, and propped up pillows to make sure she was comfortable, bringing her little tidbits of food to eat. She got Harriet to open and close her mouth a few times like a little bird, and then she would drop a little morsel in her "beak." Thankfully, Harriet felt much better in a few days the rest of us were spared from what turned out to be measles.

Chapter 17

Independence Day
July 1829

Jonathan announced one morning, early in July, "Abigail and Mariah, we need your help now to bring in more cash. You have been doing a very good job with the milking and making cheese and we appreciate that, but since Sarah is helping more with the farming this year, we need you to help make up for the loss in income from her not doing shoe uppers and William's leaving. I am going to start bringing home cotton from the mill to be picked."

Mariah said, "How are you going to bring it home if it still needs to be picked?"

"They just call it picking. I don't know why. Actually, it is cleaning it. A cotton gin gets some impurities out, but there are still many left in. So you beat on it and they fall out. My friend, John Whitin, is working on an invention of a machine that will do that, but for now, it needs to be done by hand. I will take the oxcart over to the mill every so often and bring home a couple of bales for you to clean at home. It is tedious work, but it is pretty good money. We can get six or eight cents a pound for cleaned cotton. If we don't get enough money that way, Abigail, I will see about getting work for you in the mill. I want you to be able to go to school and continue improving your penmanship, so I am hoping you and Mariah can earn enough money from the cotton picking at home in the evenings. Then you will not need to stay away from school in the day to work in the mill. Since it is still light until 8:30 or so, summertime is a good time to have evening work."

Abigail snapped, "You're not my father, you know."

I told her, "Abigail, you have just been out of sorts lately and hard to live with. No, Jonathan isn't your father. He is your older brother and is trying his best to keep this family together. Now, if you won't cooperate, we can go to Mr. Nolen and ask him what to do with you since he is our guardian. But until Father and Mother's will gets settled, we are very short of cash and we need your help."

"None of my friends have to work. I don't want to either," she said.

"Who of your friends lives in a large family with no mother or father?" I answered. "We have to do things differently because of our situation. You should be happy that we are not being auctioned off as so many orphans are."

"Stop talking to me that way," she said, stomping out of the room, running up to the garret, and slamming the door of her chamber.

"It's her age," I said. "I remember being like that when I was about twelve or thirteen. Sarah just became sulky and quiet, but I remember being sassy, too. Nancy never did get too bad."

"What should we do with her?" Jonathan asked.

"Just what we said. We can ask Mr. Nolen about it. I'm sure he will agree that you should try bringing home the bales of cotton. If she doesn't do well with that, she can work in the mill," I said. "Although with an attitude like that, they might not want her."

Jonathan asked Mr. Nolen's advice, and he agreed with Jonathan's plan. Jonathan talked to Abigail about it again later that day while I was nearby making tea.

"I just don't like being told what to do," she said. "Why didn't you ask me which thing I wanted to do instead of being so bossy?"

"I wasn't trying to be bossy. I was just telling you what needs to be done," he said.

"Well, why can't I try doing shoe uppers like Sarah did? Why do you have to treat me like such a baby?"

"I am not treating you like a baby, but you are not an adult. I didn't think you would be old enough to do shoe uppers. It seemed like harder work to me than picking cotton clean. If you want to try shoe uppers, I guess you could. I'll talk to Deacon Bachelor about it. Do you think Mariah could do it, too?" he asked.

"Why don't you ask her? It isn't very nice to make decisions for other people without asking them about it, you know," she answered.

"It also isn't very nice to act so sassy to someone who is only trying to do what is best. I am not your enemy, you know," Jonathan said. "How do you think I feel when I am working hard to keep the family together, and I have you being sassy with me about it?"

"Well, I am sorry. Just remember I am not a baby any more," she said.

Jonathan put out his hand, and she shook it and they hugged. Jonathan walked away, wiping his forehead with his handkerchief, and said "Whew!" He went outside and began chopping wood.

Deacon Bachelor, as it turned out, was looking for more people to sew shoe uppers. He was happy to let Abigail and Mariah try it. Uppers would be much less bothersome than having cotton flying around everywhere.

I told Jonathan we should consider growing silkworms in the garret like some of the neighbors were doing, but Abigail overheard me and created such a stir about worms in the garret where she was sleeping that we dropped that idea, at least for the time being.

Independence Day started out with a bang as usual. Everyone was ready for a holiday and a day off from farming, baking and working in the mill. The day before was certainly busy, though, making tarts, and getting everyone's clothes ready. It seemed strange not having William here helping Jonathan clean the musket, carrying water in, &c. We weren't making cheese that day, so Mariah and Abigail just milked* onto the ground and saved only enough to make a little pudding.

We dressed in our finest, I in my new dress and matching birthday bonnet, and we went up to Northbridge Center for the parade and speeches. I couldn't help thinking of last year when I was irritated with Mother because she continued reminding me that she was married at my age. Another year had passed, and marriage seemed even less of a possibility than it did last year. I couldn't help thinking of Abigail's remark to Cyrus and how he had laughed. It made me blush to think of it.

Harriet was at the age where she wanted to be down walking by herself, but was too tired to walk the two miles, much of it uphill. We took turns holding her, carrying the picnic supplies and tarts and were getting quite tired. There were no boys to help since Jonathan had gone early to line up with the militia.

Suddenly, from behind, we heard someone running towards us and we turned to see Cyrus.

"Do you mind if I join you lovely lassies?" he called out. "I am going to see me first Independence Day celebration up close."

Abigail yelled out, "Oh, do come join us, Cyrus." She ran to him and grabbed his arm.

We waited for him to catch up to us, and he immediately asked to carry Harriet. "You was a sick little 'un, when I saw you last. All those red spots are gone now, eh?" He jiggled her up and down, and she pulled at his hair and laughed.

He turned to me and said, "My but you do look fetching today, Betsey."

I reddened as usual and sputtered out something unintelligible but then finally smiled and thanked him. After he greeted everyone and asked Nancy how her teaching was going he began talking to me again.

"The fahmily seems well, Betsey. It must be your good cookin' and lovin' touch."

"Thank you, Cyrus, we are very well, but I can't take all the credit. We all do our part. Sarah here has been helping Jonathan with farming. Not only do Abigail and Mariah do milking and cheese, they are going to learn to sew shoe uppers. And Miranda and Lucretia keep Harriet occupied on days that they stay home from school," I said.

"You are a hard workin' lot, that you are. I suspect you keep everyone in step and supply the motherin' touch, though, Betsey," he insisted.

Abigail said, "She will make someone a good wife someday," and with that started giggling and ran off. I was mortified and kept my eyes riveted to my feet.

"I'm sure you will," he said. "She is a persistent lil' lassie, now, she is. Sisters and brothers can be such a tease. Don't let her bother you. Tis so nice for me to be with your fahmily again. I know tis hard not to have parents, but you are so blessed to have fahmily." He tickled little Harriet a bit and then put her down to let her walk awhile.

"It's so nice to see you again," Nancy said, helping to take away the awkwardness of the moment.

"Thank you, Miss Carpenter," he said. "A fahmily like yours is a treasure." Then looking right at me, he said, "I hope you won't mind if I come visit you in the future as well."

I blushed and sputtered, and then he added, "Jonathan said you could use some more help around the farm these days."

"Yes, of course," I said.

"I'm thinkin' of quittin' the job at the mill and hirin' myself out to local farmers as a day laborer to help with the harvest."

Nancy said, "You should talk to our guardian, Mr. Nolen, and see if he would be willing to hire you. I know he has been talking about hiring someone lately both for us and for his farm."

I was starting to feel light-headed and was glad that we were almost to

Northbridge Center. I didn't know what was coming over me. Cyrus noticed and helped me along by holding onto my arm. That should have helped, but only made it worse. The next thing I knew, I woke up in Abby and Nattie Parson's parlor and Nancy was giving me smelling salts and wiping my forehead with a cool cloth. She told me Cyrus had carried me there. That piece of news almost made me faint away again. She helped me sit up and gave me some lemonade to drink. After awhile, I felt nearly fine and went outdoors in time to see Jonathan marching with the militia.

Cyrus came over to see how I was doing, and I noticed some of the people acting strange and whispering. Then I remembered that Cyrus was Irish. Last year, I had felt the way many of these people did today. I hoped I could help them see that Cyrus was a hard-working friendly fellow. I suddenly felt very protective of him and determined to show everyone that I thought he was very nice even if he was Irish.

The cannons were fired, and I screamed as usual. Cyrus laughed and looked at me approvingly. Nancy began setting out a picnic and asked him to join us. Abigail and Mariah had been selling tarts most of the morning. They certainly had a different approach from Nancy or me. They very boldly approached people and asked them if they wanted tarts. Nancy and I had always stood around shyly waiting for people to come to us. I must say, they did very well. People knew we were orphans and tended to pay a little extra. This year, we made nearly three dollars. Later that day, I gave two dollars and fifty cents to Mr. Nolen and kept fifty cents for Abigail, Mariah and me to divide amongst ourselves. My part was put in the tin for the trip to go on the canal boat.

Rev. Dr. Crane came over to talk to Nancy and told her how much he had enjoyed observing her teaching this year, looking above her head most of the time he talked. He prided himself in that he had made a good choice in asking her to take the teaching position last year. He came and greeted me also and said encouraging things about how well our family was doing in spite of our tragedy, and then he turned, spat some brown tobacco juice to the side, and walked away.

"Who was that, ahem, humble soul?" Cyrus asked.

I explained that he has been the minister here for about fifty years and we began talking about the differences between Protestant ministers and Catholic priests. He was surprised that Rev. Crane had a family, owned his own land, and did farming and teaching.

"The Catholic priests don't marry. They give themselves to God alone." He explained.

I replied, "Protestant ministers prove themselves as godly leaders in their homes. How could they lead a church if they can't even lead a family?"

"Well, I can see it both ways," he said. "A wife would be a distraction," he said and smiled at me.

"A wife would be a help. God created woman to help man, and that goes for ministers as well," I argued.

"I don't wanna fight with you, miss. We are friends. Let us shake hands," he said and extended his hand.

He held onto my hand just a little longer than he needed to shake it. It was a firm, but rough hand, and I found myself wishing there was a reason to hold it even longer. I told him his hand reminded me of Father's and then told him of Father's plough-making business. I talked for some time about Father and then realized William or Jonathan had probably already told him about him.

"You already knew this. Why didn't you stop me from going on and on," I said.

"I like to hear you talk, Miss Betsey. This is the first time you and I have talked much, and I like to hear it from your point of view. William and Jonathan told me other things," he said.

Jonathan joined us then and suggested that Cyrus come with him to meet some of the other fellows from town. As soon as they left, Nancy came over close to me and teased, "God created woman to help man, eh Betsey? Did you have any particular man and woman in mind?"

"We were talking about ministers being married, and you know it," I said.

"Talking about marriage to Cyrus are you?" she continued.

"Nancy, don't you dare start it, too. I have enough to contend with in Abigail. You two are going to plant ideas in Cyrus' head that he didn't mean to be thinking about," I said.

"I think Cyrus already had those ideas planted and sprouting before we came along and just watered them a little." She then laughed and said, "Maybe we don't have to worry about young men finding us attractive even though we have a family. I heard Cyrus say he liked our 'fahmily'."

"Let me remind you that Cyrus liking our 'fahmily' and wanting to marry me are two distinctly different matters, my dear Nancy," I said.

"Well, my dear Betsey, Cyrus is clearly talking about both distinctly different matters if you would open your ears," she said.

"What should I do, Nancy?" I asked. "He is a papist, you know. Baptists can't marry Catholics even if they are hard-working, nice-looking Irish ones."

"I'm not sure why not. We should ask Deacon Whipple about it," she said.

"That would be very presumptuous of me to begin talking to Deacon Whipple about such matters when Cyrus has not proposed," I said.

"I'm sure he would be discreet and not mention the matter to anyone else. It would be far better to have come to some decision so you can decide to either encourage or discourage Cyrus, don't you think. You could tell Jonathan what you were thinking, and he could pass on the information to Cyrus to spare him any embarrassment," Nancy said.

I thought about Deacon Whipple's conversation with us in the Spring. He had said then that the best way was not always the easiest. *Oh, Lord, what is the best way? I don't know.*

Chapter 18

*Cyrus and Betsey
End of July 1829*

    Cyrus spent most of the month here, hired by Mr. Nolen. He and Jonathan slept over at the Nolen's house in order that there be no appearance of indiscretion. The farm work is so exhausting in July. Sarah does nearly as much work as they do. They hilled the corn and potatoes for several days. Deacon Whipple suggested we plant pumpkin in the same hills with the corn to keep down weeds between the corn and because by the time the pumpkin would need the sun to ripen, the corn would be finished and could be pulled up. That way, the same land could be used for two crops. He has been so helpful to us.

    Harriet went to stay with Mrs. Prentice again at least for July. During planting, I made jams and jellies from the berries that the little girls picked. Abigail was not much of a little girl any more. She did help pick the berries at first, and when I asked if she would like to help me and learn to make the jellies and jams. I must have asked in a way that pleased her for once, and she was agreeable. It was a big help to have someone helping to keep the fire going, stirring the berries so they wouldn't burn on the bottom of the pan, and then helping to ladle the hot jams into the jars. We did it outdoors, of course, so we wouldn't heat up the house any more.

Olive came over, carrying Horace on her hip. "I just followed my nose. It smells glorious. You are so ambitious. If you have a couple extra pints, I will gladly give you two cents each for them. I know you are saving for a canal boat ride."

"Oh, thank you. I do have extra. And you are so generous. I'll add the four cents to my little tin box. I hate to have you see me now; I'm such a sight," I said, pushing the sticky strands of hair back into my cap and managing to smear berry juice on my cheek at the same time.

The next day haying began and all of us, except Lucretia and Miranda, who were in school, were out in the fields helping. Jonathan and Cyrus cut the hay with their big scythes, and Abigail, Sarah, Mariah and I later raked it into piles. When it had dried sufficiently, Sarah would bring the oxcart out and drive the oxen through the fields so we could pitch the piles onto the cart, and then she would drive it back to the barn. Jonathan and Cyrus would then pitch the hay up into the loft. At the end of each day, we felt we would die of exhaustion and headache from the heat. Thankfully, most evenings, there was a cool breeze. Some days, we needed to work especially fast because rain clouds were seen on the horizon, and the hay had to be brought in before it got wet. We ate very simply on those days; exhaustion took away our appetites. We did drink plenty of lemonade, switchel and just plain water, though.

At the end of just such a day, we had thrown buckets of water at each other and had collapsed in the shade of the house. Cyrus said, "'Tis good to have land and to work on it knowin' you can keep what ya grow. I want to buy land of me own. What would you advise me to do?"

I started feeling dizzy and forced myself to take deeper breaths. This was no time to faint.

Jonathan explained again, "We can't help you because our inheritance will already be quite small when it gets divided between us all. Maybe you should move out West, where there is plenty of land and no prejudice against the Irish."

"Maybe you're right, but this New England land reminds me of the old country, and I do so wish I could stay here," he said. "Don't ya know of any friends with land to sell?"

"People are buying and selling land all the time," Jonathan explained, "but it's mainly an acre here or there, not a big enough plot for a whole new farm. Besides, the winters are so hard and the soil so rocky and the land so hilly. If I were starting from scratch like you, I would go West where I could get some decent land. Maybe you can find William and help each other out."

"For me, leavin' Ireland was adjustment enough. I feel at home now in Massachusetts, 'specially since your fahmily has befriended me. And, I like civilization. No, the West is not for me," he said.

"Are you sure you want to farm?" Jonathan continued. "Maybe you could buy up one of these acre lots and start a business of some kind or work in someone else's business. Deacon Bachelor is starting to hire people to come make shoes at his place. He said he intends to build a factory and not send so much work out any more. Maybe you could buy some land up by Northbridge Center and work for him."

"I guess I don't really know what I want yet for sure. I just know I like it here and I like your fahmily. You're like me own fahmily," he said.

Abigail said, "We like you too, don't we?" and she elbowed me in the side.

"Yes, we do. You're nearly like fahmily to us, too, though that accent of yours is a constant reminder that you're not," I said, laughingly imitating him. "I am going in to find something easy to fix for tea time. Abigail, will you come help me, too?" I asked, hoping I had said it in just the right way to please her. "Actually, all you girls need to come in and get changed out of your work dresses; I think everything we're wearing needs washed. We'll soak everything overnight in suds and do laundry tomorrow."

"Oh, all right," Abigail said, and the rest of the girls came in to change.

We bustled around the kitchen and went to the root cellar and were able to find a combination of enough leftovers to put a meal together. We were just putting out the pounded cheese, some bread, pickles, pies and cold meat, when Jonathan came in and said he would like to see me outside a minute.

He took me aside and said, "Cyrus has asked if he might start seeing you, that is, if you might want to go with him for walks and such. He didn't know what the proper approach would be since there was no father to talk to about it, and he never saw you alone to ask."

"Jonathan, I don't know what to do. If this develops into a serious relationship, what would I do? He's a papist," I said.

"Well, I can't tell you if it will develop into a serious relationship, and only you can decide if being a papist is such a bad thing. Last year, you thought being Irish was. Maybe you need to talk to Cyrus about that and see what he really believes. All I know is that he is respectable, and I would be willing for this to develop into a serious relationship, as you call it. What should I tell him?"

"Oh, I am so embarrassed. I sometimes wish there were matchmakers who would handle this sort of thing for you. I suppose he must have an answer. Well, I guess I don't need to decide on my whole future this minute. I just need to decide if I am willing to go on walks and such." I thought about it a minute more. "Yes, I am willing to do that, tell him."

At tea time, I couldn't make my eyes meet Cyrus's. Afterwards, Jonathan said he would help clean up, and Cyrus asked if we might go for a walk. I'm sure I turned a thousand shades of red, and he just laughed. "Do you mind if we don't wear shoes?" he asked.

That made me laugh and realize I had no reason to make such a big ordeal about this. "Gladly," I replied, and we both took our shoes off. We walked out to the brook by the grist mill and sat along the bank and put our feet in for awhile. The water felt so good, we decided to stay there and forget the walk. We were both too tired anyway.

"Work in the fields takes every ounce of energy," I said, "but some day when we haven't exhausted ourselves first, we can walk over to Purgatory Chasm. It is just up the French Road about a mile."

"Bein' a Catholic, I can say that goin' to Purgatory doesn't sound appealin', 'specially on a hot day," he said.

"It's just a name. I never even stop to think about it. It is a deep gorge with huge rocks you can climb over and caves to go through. Actually, it is quite cool down in there. I haven't been there for years; I might not fit in the caves any more. A beautiful piney forest surrounds it. I think you would like it," I said. "What do Catholics believe about Purgatory, anyway?" I asked, a little afraid to bring up religious topics.

"It's where your soul goes after you die, until you paid for your sins," he said.

I sat upright, startled, and thought awhile. "Why did Jesus come and die for our sins if we have to be punished for them anyway?"

"Well, maybe you didn't do enough good works to take care of the many sins you did," he said. "Or maybe you died before you got a chance to ask God to forgive you. I don't know, I'm no priest."

"Do you really believe that?" I asked.

"Well, I guess I do; I'm a Catholic, ain't I?" he answered. "But why talk about Purgatory when 'tis a beautiful day and I'm with a pretty lass coolin' my feet in the brook. You said this place you'd like to go, this chasm is on French Road. Where is that?"

"Right there, not 100 feet from where we sit," I said and pointed to the road at the corner of our property.

"What have the French to do with it?" he asked. "There are no French around these parts, are there?"

"I was afraid you would ask that," I said. I sighed and continued, "Well, over a hundred years ago, a group of French Protestants called the Huguenots came to North America from Europe when they were fleeing from the Catholics who wanted to kill them. Catholicism was the official religion, you see. The trail they took was this very road which leads to Oxford, so people started referring to it as Huguenot Road or French Road," I answered. "Father liked to read about history, so he told me about it. No one thinks about it now, any more than they think about the name Purgatory Chasm." I said, putting my head in my hands. "Why does every simple conversation we try to have turn to the differences between Catholics and Protestants?"

"I say, let's forget about the differences between the Catholics and Protestants. They're still fighting in Ireland about it, and I guess that's half of the reason why Americans don't like us Irish here, either. Can't we just be Christians?" he said. "As for you and me, can't we just be Betsey and Cyrus, not Betsey the Baptist and Cyrus the papist?"

"Well, I suppose we could," I said, not sure that I believed it.

"I think I'm a Baptist* now anyway after that dousing Jon gave me with a bucket of water," he said. He stood up, laughing and reached down to offer his hand to help me up.

I took his hand and nearly lost my breath at the same time. We started walking through the orchard. The apples were ripening and we each picked one to eat. I couldn't help but think of Adam and Eve standing there eating apples which kept me thinking about our religious differences.

Finally I said, "I can't just stop being a Baptist like it's something you turn off and on for Sabbath. It affects how I live every day. Are you just a Catholic on Sabbath days?"

"No, of course not. Actually, I hardly feel like a Catholic at all since I haven't been to confession in years."

"How do you GO to confession?" I asked, having never heard that term before.

"Sometime during the week, usually Saturday, you go to the church to the priest who is sittin' behind a curtain where you can't see each other. You tell him what you did wrong that week, and he tells you what to do about it so you'll be ready for Mass on Sunday."

"What kinds of things does he tell you to do?" I asked.

"Well, it depends on how bad your sin was. Sometimes, he tells you to say your rosary a certain number of times, or sometimes he tells you to say, 'Oh, my God I am heartily sorry for havin' offended thee, because of thy just punishment, but most of all because it offends thee. I firmly resolve with the help of thy grace to sin no more and to avoid the near occasions of sin.'"

"How did you say that so fast?" I asked. It sounded beautiful, but I could hardly understand it. Please say it again for me."

He did say it again, but found it nearly impossible to make himself say it slowly. He lost his place, when he tried.

"When you say it all your life, it's easy to say it fast," he said. "You ought to see how fast I can say the Hail, Marys." And then he demonstrated that as well.

"Why do you go to a priest to confess instead of just praying to God and asking forgiveness," I asked.

"Just sayin' it to God would be too easy. It's hard to make yourself say out loud to another person all the things ya do wrong, especially when ya confess the same things week after week. Sometimes I don't go at all 'cause I'm too ashamed."

"I know how you feel. I am ashamed confessing the same things to God over and over again, too. Rev. Bloomer says God never tires of forgiving us, though. I used to think that as you got older, you probably wouldn't sin as much, but it seems that it's just the opposite. You probably just get better at hiding it or not talking about it. That's so silly, when you think of it, because God even knows our thoughts, and they're more sinful than our actions. For instance, I have not slapped a certain person in our family yet, but I become so angry with her that I think about doing it many times."

"I'm no priest. You don't need to confess to me," he said.

"Well, the Bible says you're supposed to confess your sins to one another. If you went by what you saw me do, maybe you would think I never get angry. So, I'm just telling you I do."

"Well, as long as we are confessin'. I confess that you are pretty, and I think you are very nice, and that I think it is good that when you feel like slapping a certain fahmily member, you don't do it," he said.

I felt the red color go up my neck and my nose began to tingle. It was so much easier to talk about religion than to be told I was pretty. I wanted to tell him he was handsome and that I liked him very much, but I couldn't say a thing. I just coughed a little and began pulling up blades of grass slowly, one by one, and chewing the white ends off of them.

Cyrus bent over and scooped a handful of water in his hand and threw it at me. I retaliated, and soon we were both laughing and thoroughly drenched. He announced that he for sure was a Baptist by now, and we went back to the house arm-in-arm.

Chapter 19

Another Letter from William
End of August 1829

We received another letter from William. Maybe leaving was the right thing for him to do. His letter sounded so fine and was written on clean paper with a real envelope.

"August 18, 1829

Dear Family,

"I am well and hope you are, too. I went past Ohio to Illinois. Betsey or Nancy, do you still have your geography textbook? You could look at the map of the Northwest Territory and see most of what I describe. I got to Pittsburgh. What a busy place! You wouldn't believe what a big city it is. There must be 20,000 people there. It is down in a river valley surrounded by mountains. I first saw it from atop Third Brother Mountain. Two big rivers called Monongahela and Allegheny meet to form the Ohio River. It is quite a sight, and houses as far as you can see on the river banks. I found a young family that was looking for another person to help them navigate their flatboat down the Ohio. They had theirs already built using some of the lumber from their covered wagon for part of it. It is like a little house on top of a rectangular boat. We stood on top of the flat roof of the house to steer with our long poles. We had to be on the lookout for snags, which are trees that had fallen in the river, and sandbars. It was tricky.

"Sometimes, if we saw a settlement, we stopped along the shore to visit for awhile with settlers. We heard our share of stories of boats that got torn apart from snags in the river. Sometimes, we went ashore and bought supplies. Other times, we would tie up to shore and just get a good night's rest. We caught a lot of fish and usually cooked them on board in a sort of kitchen so we could travel as much as possible during daylight. We kept chickens on board so always had fresh eggs which was nice. Sometimes they would get out and fly off onto another passing boat, though, and we would have to fetch them back.

"I never paid attention to geography in school, so I was surprised to find out that the Ohio River flowed West. I thought all rivers flowed South, I guess since South is at the bottom of a map and rivers flow down. The Ohio does flow South some, but mainly West. I never imagined I would pass by so many states on one river. We started in Pittsburgh, Pennsylvania, like I said. After awhile, the Ohio River is the border between states. On the right bank was Ohio and our left was West Virginia. Later, on our left was Kentucky, and half-way through Kentucky, Indiana was then on our right bank. Then, after weeks of floating on this river, we met the mighty Mississippi River in Cairo, Illinois! I only agreed to go with the family as far as the Mississippi River. They wanted to continue on South so had to find someone else to help them. I wonder if we will ever meet again. Probably not. They had three little girls, so I felt right at home with them.

"I am now near Cairo which is the southern-most tip of Illinois. South of me is Kentucky and Tennessee and West of me on the other side of the Mississippi is Missouri. My age has been a big help. I am strong enough to be of help but not old enough that they expect me to know what to do (which is good since I don't). I am also young enough that they still feel sorry for me not having any parents but old enough that I can help those with young families. Little children especially like me and surround me, pulling on my legs and arms. My arms are even stronger now from all the rowing and poling (and tugging from the children).

"I don't know what I will do next. Here I am, and now what? You would be surprised at how much I talk to people. I seem to have left my shyness somewhere back in Connecticut or New York. I plan to talk to a lot of people and get some ideas. Maybe I will stay here. Maybe I will look for land eventually. I have been thinking of selling my part of Father's land if the will ever gets settled. Then I would have money to buy land here. I need to look around for awhile first anyway and be sure. For now, I am working on a farm. I still have Father's plough handles, which I thought I would have lost by now. I don't know why I brought them; they still make me cry to hold them.

"Please be happy for me, even though I miss you terribly when I have time to think of it. If you get this letter and write to me soon to the post office in Cairo, Illinois, I will probably be around here for a month or so but I don't know how long the mail will take.

Love, William

PS How's Cyrus?"

Immediately, everyone started thinking about Cyrus buying William's property, and the will was not yet even probated. We all felt like vultures. It wasn't right that it almost made us hope William would not come back so Cyrus could buy his land.

We borrowed a piece of paper from Mr. and Mrs. Nolen and all wrote a section of a letter to William. It was interesting to read each other's sections to see what each person thought was important. Writing to him also made us stop our work long enough to remember how much we missed him. We had to all write extremely small and use front and back to make it fit on our one piece of paper. I began:

"Dear William,

I hope this letter reaches you in Cairo. We were very upset when you left and were tempted to send someone to find you, but realized you needed to go. Your geography lesson was very interesting, and as I read your letter, I could picture you on the roof of the flatboat steering with a pole, with three little girls pulling at your legs and a chicken flying off the boat. I hope you are keeping a journal. Some day you will have children who will enjoy reading of their father's adventures when he was young. I wish you could taste some of the jams we just made. Betsey"

Sarah came over to write, stared at the page awhile and said she needed more time.

Abigail then continued, using her best penmanship,

> "I helped make the jams. Betsey is a slave driver. I now make cheese as well. Another calf was born the night you left. Both calves are doing fine. Can you tell that I am learning penmanship? It takes a long time to write this way, but it makes me feel like an artist. Abigail"

Mariah and Miranda then added,

> "I miss you. I work much harder since you left. I make cheese, too. Mariah"
>
> Hi. This is Miranda. How are you? I am fine. I still teach Lucretia everything, so she is learning to write her letters and do her sums. I miss you. Love, Miranda."

In big wavy letters, Lucretia wrote,

> "I mis you. War ar you? Wen wil you com bak? Wuz the bot fun? Hoo do you liv wif? I lost four toofs. I mis you. LUCRETIA"

She then drew a picture of a face with tears coming down the cheeks and drew an arrow from her name to the face.

Jonathan wrote,

> "Dear William,
>
> We are so busy as usual for July and August. I work most days on the farm and seldom work in the mill. We miss you. We have hired Cyrus as a day laborer. He and I sleep at Mr. and Mrs. Nolen's so our house if for 'ladies' only. Deacon Whipple showed us a new trick of planting pumpkins in the same hills with the corn. You might want to try that, too. The canal has been very busy. The mills are having their cotton shipped up that way now. It is much cheaper. Leather hides for shoes and boots, too. Deacon Bachelor plans to start a manufactory for shoes up on the county road near his place up past the meeting house. He says that's better than having people sew the uppers and do the bottoming in their homes. Seems as though more and more, people won't be able to work at home. It doesn't seem right. Jonathan"

Sarah then came and sat with the quill in hand a long time and then finally dipped it in the inkwell and wrote:

> "Dear William, I can't tell you how much I miss you. I came home as soon as I found out you left. Your 'boys' are fine. Even in Rehoboth, they had heard the reputation of Sutton oxen from a farmer's magazine. I curry them well every day and make them mind. You trained them well. I am starting to train the calf you delivered; I have it pulling some light loads. I work as hard as the men during the day but do some simple mending at night to remind myself I am a girl. I gave up on shoe uppers when summer came. I haven't had time for reading much lately and no energy for reading aloud anyway. I miss having things the way they were when you were home. I would be so happy if you came back, but in some ways I admire the way you struck out to try something new. I pray for you every day while I curry the 'boys' and hope our Creator keeps you in good health. Love, Sarah"

We kept the letter for the weekend so Nancy could add to it when she came home for Sabbath. She sat down to write three times before she actually got anything down on paper. At last she wrote, stopping many times:

> "I hope you are prospering, but I must say, our family misses its other man around here. I feel bad when I see Sarah working in the fields even though she does so without complaining. William, you are family and you signed a document saying you would help us. Then you left taking some of our money. Even though it was money you earned, the paper you signed said all the money you earned would go to the family. We are all working hard to help the whole family, not just ourselves. I must confess I feel angry about your leaving and thinking only of yourself. Your family is paying in sweat for you to have an adventure. I hope your conscience will remind you of your obligation to us. I love you, too. It is hard for me to write this. It would be easier not to write it, but the easy way isn't always best. I thought I had done you a favor by working extra hard so you could work on the canal, but when you saw we could work that hard, you came to expect it all the time from us. It isn't right. Nancy."

She got up, breathing deeply, and wiped tears from her eyes.

"Nancy, I can hardly believe what I read," I said. "I knew you were angry with William when he first left, but I didn't know you still felt that way. Are you sure you want him to read that? Think how melancholy he is by nature any way."

"I know he is melancholy, but he can't use that as an excuse to get his own way at the expense of everyone else. He has to learn to carry his share of the load. I love him, too, but I don't think you do him a favor by letting him be thoughtless," she answered.

Cyrus added a line,

> "William, I hope you find time for a game of rounders now and then. If you decide to sell your land, I know of an interested person. Cyrus."

On our walk on Monday, we went to Mr. Cheney Taft's store to post the letter. I sometimes saw people whispering about us, but I didn't care. I knew Cyprus's character, and they did not.

Cyrus had been working on our farm regularly. Any cash that we earned went to the estate and Mr. Nolen used it to pay Cyrus. I was surely glad now for Mr. Nolen's guardianship; it would have been very awkward for me or Jonathan to pay Cyrus.

He sometimes attended Sabbath meeting with us but could hardly sit still during one of our services and was not used to the congregational singing. He also mentioned that he missed Mass being said in Latin, that Latin seemed more religious and he had a million questions about why we did things the way we did.

One week, the Lord's Supper was served, and Rev. Bloomer spoke to Cyrus ahead of time and asked him if he believed in Jesus as his personal Savior. Cyrus didn't know exactly what he meant by that but said he wouldn't partake anyway because he had not been to confession and besides, Catholics were strictly forbidden to partake in a Protestant church.

I asked him, "Why can't you take communion in our church?"

He said, "Protestants only believe the bread and juice to be symbols, but Catholics believe they miraculously become the body and blood of Christ. You are thought to be heretics."

We didn't talk any further about it. I thought about what it would be like to think you were actually eating Christ's body and drinking his blood. At first, the thought sickened me. Then I remembered that food becomes a part of you when you eat it, and it is what keeps you alive. By eating Christ's body, we make him a part of us, and he gives us life. *It's so true. You do give us life. Thank you, Lord. I do need you more than food or drink.*

Chapter 20

Cyrus and I Make Plans
September 1829

Cyrus and I continued to go for walks each day, and we started avoiding religious topics more and more and talked instead about crops, weather, how times were changing, &c. One day, he seemed unusually out of sorts and I asked him what was the matter.

"The matter, my dear lass, Betsey, is that I love you very much. How much longer can I go on talking about the weather when I want instead to make you me wife."

This statement took my breath away and any good sense I might have had. My mind felt like applesauce. I looked at this handsome Irishman beside me and admitted to myself that that was what I wanted, too, but I couldn't just come out and say it like he could.

So, taking my hands in his, he turned his statement into a question, "Betsey, my dear Betsey, would you consider bein' me wife?"

My eyes filled up with tears and my throat tightened and I nodded my head, unable to speak. He then kissed me gently on the forehead.

Our walks in the next days became planning sessions for a wedding. We didn't tell the family, but we were sure they would all be happy. We were waiting for just the right time. It seemed so easy, really. We would be married in a simple ceremony in our home, and Cyrus would move in with us, and when the will was probated, we would build a house on the land I inherited. The Nolens had come to like him, too, since he had been staying with them. I was sure they would be happy for us.

I felt wonderful knowing that someone loved me enough to want to spend the rest of his life with me, and he felt wonderful knowing that he would finally have a "fahmily" and a place to settle. One beautiful September day, we decided to file our intention to marry with the town clerk. We planned to surprise the family soon afterward with our plan, although, we both were so happy around each other, I was sure it would come as no surprise.

The next day, I suggested that we take a walk to Deacon Whipple's house who lived only about a half-mile away. He was so kind, and I was sure, as Justice of the Peace, he would be willing to perform the wedding ceremony in our home when the time came. I introduced them, and they began talking about the beautiful countryside, and soon we were talking about our land.

"Since you young people like taking walks so much, you might want to take a walk up to the land that Betsey will inherit some day," he said. "I don't remember which parcel exactly is hers. It's been years since I helped your father write his will, but I remember it is part of the Estey lot off of French Road, up Rocky Road a piece. It's a nice piece of woodland—too rocky for farming, but a beautiful piece of land none the less—a good source of firewood and a nice place for an evening walk."

"I am surprised," I said, nearly breathless. "I always assumed I would inherit part of the land suitable for farming."

"Oh, no, I'm very sure of that," he answered. "I may have mislead you when we talked of it earlier. I'm sorry. The farmland all goes to William and Jonathan, and it will be several years yet before William is old enough to inherit his land. Isn't he only fifteen or so?"

"You mean that even when the will gets probated, only the ones that are twenty-one can claim their inheritance?" I asked.

"Yes, that's right," he answered, "unless Mr. Nolen agrees to let him sell it."

"That will be a disappointment for William," I said. "He was beginning to think about selling his land so he could buy something in Illinois or Ohio. I wish he had talked to you first before he left. Well, we must be going. Good-bye."

"It was a pleasure to meet you, Cyrus. I understand you have been indispensable to Mr. Nolen and the Carpenters. You canal workers are used to putting in a good hard day of labor."

"We always got a jigger of rum now and then on the canal, though. Betsey and Jonathan only allow me water and switchel," Cyrus said, laughing.

"You seem to be surviving," Deacon Whipple said. "You're none the worse for it, I'm sure."

"Yes, sir. Well, 'twas a pleasure to meet you as well," Cyrus said.

As we walked back home, both of us were silent for a long time. Finally, I said, "I wish I had talked to Deacon Whipple about this before, as well. I am feeling very young and foolish."

Cyrus was clearly shaken as well. "I am the young and foolish one. I wanted to marry you so bad, I didn't find out the facts."

Chapter 21

Our Plans Change

Soon after receiving William's letter, another letter arrived which was to completely change our future. Cyrus received a letter from an Irish friend that he had worked with on the Blackstone Canal, who now lived in a section of Worcester for the Irish, called Green Island, and had a job with a wire company. He asked Cyrus to come visit.

Cyrus wanted me to come along, too, but since I didn't know anyone in Worcester and certainly could not have stayed in the home of his unmarried friend, I didn't go. Nancy and I decided that this would be as good a time as any, to take our trip south along the Blackstone Canal to Providence, Rhode Island. We counted the money in the little tin, however, and found we were still twenty cents short.

Cyrus left the house and returned later with thirty-five cents which he insisted we use for the trip and to buy something special. I gave him a big hug, and he smiled broadly and said, "The hug was well worth the thirty-five cents. I shouldn't have waited so long to give it to you."

Lucretia watched all this, then disappeared into her bedchamber and returned with a penny. "I found thith next week. You can have it for your trip."

I gave her a hug, too, and told her I think she found it last week. "I'll buy you a treat in Providence. Maybe some false teeth, you little grandma." She laughed.

Abigail then proudly brought out three cents she had been saving and said to get something for the family. I think Cyrus's and Lucretia's generosity had worn off on her a little. She was obviously pleased to have money of her own to contribute.

Olive Nolen said she would watch over the family. The two of us made plans including an overnight stay of two nights in Providence with the same family where Sarah had stayed, Rebecca Bradford's parents.

We started the trip at the same place where we had watched the opening of the canal last autumn, the day Mother took ill, over by the Capron Mill in Uxbridge. In fact, we rode on the same canal boat, a packet called *Lady Carrington* and both of us felt like ladies a little bit, and a little bit like children that day. Everyone seemed to notice us and smile, and I don't think I have ever smiled as much as I did on that journey. Everything we saw and did seemed delightful or hilariously amusing. Being with Nancy was the most wonderful fun.

Almost immediately after we embarked on this voyage of ours, the canal went over an aqueduct so that we could cross over the Mumford River, which was about twenty-five feet below us. It was an eerie feeling knowing that we were so far up in the air. I had to remind myself that it was not much different than being on a bridge; instead of a road over the bridge, however, we were in a wooden trench of water being pulled by horses on a path beside us. An old man by the name of Mr. Hosken was on this trip with us, and he seemed to know everything about every community along the way, so we received a liberal education, which we both enjoyed. We began to realize just how isolated we were, growing up only knowing about Sutton, Northbridge, Uxbridge and Douglas.

We soon passed some lovely farm land, and the house on it, owned by Bezaleel Taft, was enormous. He had landscaped part of it with unusual shrubs and trees. I couldn't imagine living in so large a house.

Mr. Hosken said, "Mr. Bezaleel Taft was instrumental in getting legislation drafted and finding financing for the canal. He is one of the richest men in Uxbridge."

We also passed by many mills and mill villages and Mr. Hosken told us one was the Alexander Wilson scythe manufactory, but mainly they were cotton and woolen mills. There was one that was on an island in the middle of the river. It made buttons out of seeds from sycamore trees.

"Oh, look." Nancy pointed up to several little girls looking out the windows of one of the mills we passed, waving at us. "Poor things. I would have hated to be cooped up in one of those hot mills working from sunup until sundown. Many of them never go to school."

Some of the mill housing was built right on the banks of the canal on the opposite side from the tow path.

Mr. Hosken said, "When there are no canal boats in sight, the children use the canal for swimming. Last winter, they skated on it, too. I'm sure it won't be long before we will hear of drowning of a little one. Already, on a moonless night, one poor man, saturated with ardent spirits, fell in and drowned. Of course, that could have happened in the river as well."

The canal left the river and rejoined it several times. Sometimes you could see the river nearby, and other times it was nowhere in sight. Another interesting thing that happened was that the towpath would change which side of the canal it was on. That happened several times on our "voyage." Each time that happened, the horses had to cross a bridge in front of the boat to get to the other side and then the ropes would have to be attached to the other side of the boat.

At one point, right before the state boundary to Rhode Island, the river was going through such a deep gorge that canal had to go instead through a pond and then through three locks, one right after another. We went through about twenty locks altogether on our voyage. Each one took about five minutes, and each time, we went into the lock at a high level, the gates closed behind us, then water was let out through an opening in the gates in front of us. We felt the boat sink down in the lock until the water level was as low as the water level on the other side of the front gates. Then two of the crew men would open the front gates, one from each side of the canal, the ropes were reattached to the horses along the tow path, and the horses would once again pull us gently down the canal. It was most ingenious, and I never tired of it. At one lock, we were delayed because the lock tender had to remove rocks that some vandals had dropped in front of the gate.

Mr. Hosken explained, "The mill owners are unhappy about the canal because it diverts water from the river that the mill needs to run its water wheels. The canal owners, on the other hand, claim the canal helps business by supplying low cost transportation for the products the mills are making. There are often fights about it, and mill operatives have sued the canal or dropped rocks in the locks, and canal workers allegedly set fires to the mills."

In Rhode Island, we passed a wharf that was covered with a fine white powder, and there were there piles of casks waiting for another canal boat.

"What is that white powder all over the ground?" I asked.

Mr. Hosken explained, "It is lime from the limestone at the Dexter Lime Company. They use it for cement that is so good it even works under water. In fact, it had been used to build the locks for the canal."

"Oh, yes, I remember seeing some of those same casks the day William and I watched the lock being built over by Goat Hill," I said.

After that, we passed through quite a large pond called Scott's Pond. Mr. Hosken told us, "Its depth had to be raised twelve feet because of the canal, and when that was done, some of the trees and cranberry bushes became dislodged from the land and formed a floating island. You never know on what part of the pond you will find it. There are mysterious stories about this floating island."

Then, we actually left the Blackstone River, or it left us. I don't know which. It continued over the Pawtucket Falls and to Narragansett Bay, and we instead went through a half-mile long cut in a hillside and joined the Moshassuck River and followed it and the canal into the center of Providence. At one point, the Smithfield Turnpike crossed the canal, and we waved to a farmer driving an oxcart over the bridge above us.

Occasionally, we would pass another canal boat going North to Worcester. We saw one carrying mostly lumber, shingles and tools. Another carried bales of cotton. Another had tons of hides—probably, for the shoe manufacturing in Northbridge and Grafton. Another had furniture, and others had hundreds of bushels of corn, barrels of molasses and an assortment of bushels and barrels of this and that. It was most interesting. We arrived in Providence before sunset and bid a friendly good-bye to our new friend, Mr. Hosken.

I had never been to a big city before, and was amazed at the activity of thousands of people in one street after another, busy in various activities in shops of all kinds. I could not have imagined so many horses and carriages all in one place. Only a short distance away was the State House with its gold-domed roof and also Salt Cove, where big merchant ships were docked.

Mr. Bradford was waiting for our arrival and quickly took us by surrey to his home. Other than the time we rode with Mother when she was sick a year ago, we had never ridden in one before. Mr. and Mrs. Bradford spoke of Sarah's overnight stay with them, and I told them of her misfortune after she left them, when the stagecoach wheel fell off, and she was caught in a rain storm. It was laughable now, since it all turned out for the best.

The next day, we returned to Providence to see the sights. Mrs. Bradford told us we simply must see the Arcade which was just built last year. It was indeed amazing. We walked in a door on one street and walked through an enclosed mall with shops on either side three stories high, and kept walking for one whole city block with continuous shops the whole way. In these shops were wares from every country of the world, I can well imagine, even silks and tableware from China. Nancy and I each indulged in one extravagance. I bought a scarf, and she a collar, and we bought little sweetmeats for the children and Jonathan and Cyrus.

After leaving the Arcade, we walked down to the wharf and saw the mighty merchant ships. It was from these ships that all the goods came for the shops in the Arcade. They had giant masts, rigged for many sails. We could see one off the coast with its enormous sails billowing out. The sight was thrilling. If William had seen these, he would have signed on immediately, I'm sure.

We stayed for some time breathing the salt air and letting the cool sea breeze blow our long dresses around. This was our first time seeing the ocean. We stood in silence, each one dreaming her own dream as the seagulls soared up in the blue sky, cawing. I dreamed of Cyrus and me sailing off to an island by ourselves. Then I remembered Nancy beside me and decided I really didn't want to leave the family behind.

Nancy interrupted my reverie. "Look at those black, long-necked birds standing on the mossy rock over there. Why do you think they stand like that with their wings outspread?"

A male voice behind us answered, "Those are cormorants, and they are drying their wings. Watch them, and you'll see them go diving for fish."

"Mr. Cooper, what are you doing here? I had just been thinking how strange it was to be surrounded by people and not to have made the acquaintance of a single one, and then you come along," I said.

"I come down to the shore every Monday, Wednesday and Friday as soon as my passengers get off the stagecoach and I have delivered the bag of mail I have picked up from the towns between Worcester and Providence. I like to come down here to the dock and breathe in the salt air and watch the birds. Look at the seagulls picking up clams from the shallow water then flying up and dropping them on the rocks below to break them open. Then they fly down quickly to devour the tasty clam meat before one of the other gulls on the ground beats them to it."

"You are indeed fortunate to come here so often," I replied.

"I enjoy it, but it means I'm away from the wife and children much of the time."

"You should bring them along," Nancy said.

"I do sometimes if I don't have enough paying passengers. It looks like we're going to have some weather," he said pointing to the dark clouds on the horizon. "This is hurricane season, you know."

Nancy and I looked at each other. "No, we didn't know. The hurricanes don't come inland, so we're not aware of them."

"Well, you may get to see one tonight," he said, rubbing his cheeks and chin. "How did you young ladies get down here? The canal?"

"Yes, Mr. Cooper. And it was wonderful," Nancy said.

"I hope you are prepared to stay awhile, because I'm sure neither man nor beast will want to be out for a couple of days if those clouds are what I think they are."

"Oh, no. We have no way of telling our family," I said.

"If I hear tell of someone leavin' on horseback yet this afternoon, I'll give him the message."

"Oh, thank you, Mr. Cooper. That would be so kind of you."

"Well, good day, ladies. I hope you enjoy your stay. Where are you lodging?"

"At Miss Bradford's parents' house. She is one of the school mistresses in Northbridge," Nancy answered. "She and I are friends."

"Yes, of course. I have heard of her. She's the one that brought in that Methodist minister from Providence. They're having meetings now in Rufus Bennett's house, ain't they?"

"Yes," Nancy answered. "I attended several meetings this past winter when the weather was too severe for me to go home for Sabbath observance. They were very fine. The congregation is small, of course, but they are very sincere Christians, and I have benefited each time I attended."

"Well, I don't know that we need new religions. Seems to me that when everyone was Congregational, it was just fine. But then you're all Baptists, anyway, ain't you?"

"Yes, we are members of South Sutton Second Baptist Church," I said, thinking about Cyrus saying, "Why can't you be just plain Betsey instead of Betsey the Baptist."

"Enough talk about church. I need to be on my way. Let's hope that hurricane won't be too bad. Good day, ladies."

"Good day, Mr. Cooper."

"We probably should leave the dock, too, if we want to see the rest of Providence," I said.

We left with a big sigh, looking again to the south where the dark clouds were on the horizon. We walked past mansions where the governor and several merchants lived, and looked in briefly at the meeting house of the first Baptist church in America. Roger Williams started it almost two hundred years ago, though the building is only fifty years old. There was the most beautiful, huge chandelier, and a pulpit such as we had in our South Sutton Baptist church which had stairs to climb so that the minister could be seen by all. After that, we left the busy downtown section and climbed a hill to see Brown University. We stopped for a cup of tea in one of the inns and then began the long walk back to the Bradford's house.

Neither of us was accustomed to wearing shoes for so long of a walk, but since we had not seen anyone else barefooted, we kept them on the whole time. Our feet were considerably sore when we got back, so we soaked them and then took a nap, thankful to have our feet up.

At tea time, Mr. and Mrs. Bradford's son, Stephen, who works at the Customs House, joined us. Hearing him talk about the merchant ships from all around the world was so interesting. I suddenly realized how Sarah must have felt staying in another town for six weeks and not knowing how she would ever come back to the farm.

"Tell us about your farm," Stephen said wistfully. "How much land do you own?"

"I don't know exactly," I answered. "We have a few acres of apple orchard, a couple acres of corn and rye, a vegetable garden, and several acres of woodland. We have a couple of cows and oxen, some pigs, and chickens. Nothing big. Our father had a small plough-making business in our home, so farming was something he did on the side."

"Nancy told us that both your parents passed away. It must be a challenge keeping up with the farm work," Mrs. Bradford said.

"Yes, it is. We had to hire some help, actually, since one of our brothers moved out West and the other one works many days in a cotton mill," I said. I could feel myself blushing.

Nancy added, "We hired an Irish young man who had helped to build the canal. He is a hard worker, and he likes our family very much. Especially Betsey." At this, we both burst out laughing.

Stephen looked a little disappointed, I thought. It may have been my imagination, though.

"What is a typical day for you on the farm?" he asked.

"Nancy teaches school, so she lives with the families of the scholars. But for me, it's the usual making of breakfast, getting the children up and dressed and off to school. Abigail and Mariah do the milking before they leave, and then I usually make cheese, do laundry, and make a nooning. The school is close enough for the children to come home and eat at noon. In the afternoon, I do sewing, and whatever seasonal things there are to do like making soap, candles, weaving, &c. Soon, it will be time to pick apples, so we will keep the girls home from school to help with that. Then, we'll slice some of them and dry them. Nothing very exciting," I said.

"It may not be exciting, but it certainly sounds inviting to be out of doors picking apples instead of sitting in an office in a noisy city," he said.

"Well, you all must come up and visit us sometime. I would recommend the trip up the canal. It is slow but very relaxing. Otherwise, you could catch a stage. It comes through from Providence to Worcester every other day. A friend of our family's from Northbridge is the stagecoach driver. In fact, we saw him down at the dock today," I said.

Even as I issued the invitation, I hoped they wouldn't accept because I felt they couldn't possibly appreciate our simple life, and I felt a bit ashamed of it. Their house was so neat and clean and nicely furnished. They had a wash basin and pitcher in each chamber. No one washed in the kitchen as we did. They ate with forks and had a separate room just for eating.

Nancy added, "Mr. Cooper, the stagecoach driver, said he predicted some stormy weather soon. What do you think?"

Mr. Bradford said, "It is the season for it, but often the storms turn out to sea before they reach us. We always hope that will happen. Otherwise, you young ladies may be staying a little longer than you anticipated."

Mrs. Bradford said, "And I would be happy for your company if you do; though, I'm sure if the storm comes, we won't be going out anywhere."

Nancy looked over at the bookcase and said, "If we do stay, I think I will indulge in some reading. I'm not used to having a choice of books so readily available."

Mr. Bradford said, " Stephen, I think you and I had better close the shutters on the house tonight or we may not have any windows left in the morning."

Both of us were trying hard to conceal our yawns and finally just admitted we needed to go to bed early. It was good that we did, because that early sleep was all that we got. By midnight, the wind began to blow fiercely.

The whole house began to rattle and creak and we could hear the wind blowing through the trees in the yard, though we couldn't see a thing because of the shutters. Every once in awhile we would hear a branch crack and fall and occasionally feel a branch get blown against the house. Then the rain began. Mrs. Bradford came up to our chamber and suggested that we dress and come down to the parlor so we could all be together.

We went down and all sat around a flickering whale oil lamp. The sound of the wind and rain was so loud, we couldn't hold a conversation. At one point, a sudden gust of wind blew the front door open. It took all of us to push it shut, and Mr. Bradford bolted it. That was our first sight of the outdoors. The rain was coming down almost horizontal. The street in front of the house was a swirling river. Mrs. Bradford grabbed a rag and wiped up the rain on the floor.

Hours passed, and the wind blew and battered the house, and it rained continually. Mrs. Bradford screamed, "The water is coming in under the door. Quick, pull up the rugs and get them upstairs."

We scurried around, moving furniture off the rugs. Then Stephen and Mr. Bradford quickly rolled them up and carried them up the stairs to the chamber where we had been sleeping.

"We might as well take some of this smaller furniture up as well and if the flooding gets worse, maybe we'll bring the bigger stuff up, too," Mr. Bradford said.

"There's no sense in us staying down here, getting our feet wet. We could at least sit on the stairs," Stephen said. "And let's pray for God's protection instead of sitting here fearful like a bunch of heathens."

He prayed briefly, and I couldn't help but think how nice it was for a young man to do that. I wondered if Cyrus would, but decided he wouldn't. It might only because he wasn't used to such a thing, though. We Baptists and Methodists were.

It seemed as if morning would never come, and when it did, it was still storming so badly, and the shutters were still covering the windows, so it remained dark in the house. Mr. Bradford and Stephen were unable to go to work of course, so we sat around reading and visiting the whole day.

Stephen taught me to play chess while Nancy read. It was like having an older cousin. After he won three games, we stopped and talked about our ambitions. He wanted to continue working in finance somehow and find someone who would help him understand investments.

"The most important thing, though, is to do God's will and be honest. I pray every day that I will desire for His kingdom to come and His will to be done above any ambitions I may have," he said.

"I used to pray that, too, but have been negligent lately," I said. "I'm glad you have reminded me of it." I made a mental note to talk to Cyrus about this.

By late afternoon, the storm had "blown out to sea" as they say here. Stephen and Mr. Bradford opened the shutters again and began picking up fallen branches and debris.

The next morning, Mr. Bradford walked over to the terminus for the canal to see if it would be open today and the boats running. They said it would, so Nancy and I packed our bags to go home. It was hard to leave. We felt like family by this time.

The return trip home was slower because the captain often had to stop to clean out fallen branches from the canal and tow path. We didn't pay as much attention to the sights. Instead, we again talked about our futures, and Nancy and I had our first long talk about Cyrus.

"Tell me all about Cyrus," she said. "You have gotten to know him much better since I left home."

All of the sudden, I realized I didn't know very much about Cyrus at all. "Well, you know Cyrus. He is very nice, a hard worker, uh, Irish, and you know he is a Catholic," I answered.

"I think it is more important to talk about his faith in God than if he is a Catholic," she said. "Is religion just a formality to him? Some Catholics, I hear, are just born and baptized that way, and that's all their religion is. They just know they are Catholic and not Protestant, but they don't know what it means. Others are very sincere and devout in their faith. The same with Protestants; some just go to meeting because everyone expects it. Does he really believe in God and does he believe that Jesus died on the cross so that he might be forgiven of his sins if he is truly repentant?"

"I think so," I said. "He is a very good person. We have such different ways of believing, after awhile, we stopped talking about them. They didn't seem that important. We do enjoy being together."

"You said you were starting to get serious about him. What do you mean by that?" she asked.

"It's as you told the Bradfords. He likes our family, me especially. And you know he likes living on a farm and would like to own some land near us," I answered. I couldn't bring myself to tell her the truth.

"What is his family like? How old is he? Are you talking about marriage? Can he support a family?" she asked.

"So many questions," I answered. "I don't know all the answers. He is just hard working and means well. He doesn't talk much about his family. What does it matter how old he is? I never asked. Probably my age."

"When Mother married Father, he owned land already and had a plough-making business and was about ten years older than her, and they went to the same meeting house. I think that has a lot to do with why their marriage was so good," she said. "That's what I want to do. I want to marry someone who understands my faith and who is stable. And, of course, he must be kind and hard-working as Cyrus is. I wouldn't mind if he were as handsome as Cyrus, either," she added.

"I don't understand why you are coming up with all of these questions. I thought you liked Cyrus. You used to seem happy for me to have someone interested in me," I said.

"I think moving from one house to another in the homes of my scholars has opened my eyes. I know our family hasn't been perfect, but not like the unpleasantness that goes on in many homes, and I keep trying to figure out why so I can avoid it when I marry. I'm sure, in each case, a man and a woman start out with love and good intentions, but soon, hard times, bad health, or just plain selfishness changes things. It seems that the best marriages are where the husband and wife both love God sincerely and can talk about their faith and pray together about things. It's just not as good when one has faith and the other tries to figure everything out without faith."

I felt tears come to my eyes and my throat tighten. "I guess Cyrus and I just talk about religion, mainly, instead of real faith in God. I am glad we took a few days and left home behind for awhile. I can see our situation in a different way. I feel like I am another person looking at myself. Ever since Mother died, I have been feeling like a mother with no husband, especially in the winter months when Jonathan stayed in Northbridge most of the time. I didn't want to abandon my children, and I was looking for a man to come and complete the picture. Cyrus has been the only one to show me attention, and he likes our family so well, so I thought it was only natural that he was the missing puzzle piece. It would be a storybook ending; we would get married and share our land, and everything could return as it had been before Mother and Father died. I wanted so badly for him to be the one and for it to work out easily, so I stopped asking him any questions that he could possibly give wrong answers to. Besides, I wanted to prove to our community that I was not prejudiced against the Irish."

Nancy said, "I am not saying that he isn't the missing puzzle piece, but you need to get to know him better to be sure. You need to ask some more questions and not try to make the answers be what you want them to be, because life isn't a storybook. What if an Irish priest moved to Sutton and Northbridge? Cyrus would probably want his children to be Catholic. Do you even know what that means? I don't. You need to talk about that. Marriage is for the rest of your life, and you don't want to make a mistake in it. And you surely must not marry anyone just to prove you're not prejudiced."

"Nancy, you could be a minister if you were just a man Talking to you is like talking to Deacon Whipple. You see things so clearly and speak the truth in such a kind way. I would resent it if anyone but you or Deacon Whipple said it."

I realized that I was not ready to be married to Cyrus just yet. I had not really sincerely prayed about our marriage nor had we tried to make reasonable plans. We had just let things progress without much questioning, thinking our love for one another would make it work. I had enjoyed the touch of his hands, his gentle kisses, his love of our family, his Irish accent, but we had never talked about what really mattered, our faith in God and what we wanted our marriage to be like. Maybe eventually it will work, but not just yet. Not in three weeks. He was the only young man I had gotten to know well, and I had been in too much of a hurry. *Lord, forgive me and help me to know how to talk to Cyrus about this.*

We got off the canal boat in Uxbridge, took off our shoes and bonnets, and walked the seven miles or so home barefooted. The closer we got, the more ready we were to be home. The children saw us coming down the road and came running toward us. I felt so different in some ways, I almost didn't expect them to recognize me.

Mrs. Prentice was there with little Harriet who ran so fast to me and grabbed my legs tightly. Lucretia took one of my hands and one of Nancy's and began swinging herself between them.

"Betthee and Nanthee; you're home," she said. "I was afraid you wouldn't come home."

Had it only been four days? Our little farm even looked different. Jonathan had cut down the stalks in the corn field, and hundreds of pumpkins, starting to turn orange, were showing their heads as far as you could see. It was good to be able to see the wide open field again, the brook, and nearly up to Burt's pond.

"Let's go to the grist mill," I said. We dragged ourselves to the brook behind the mill, and put our feet in the cool water. The crisp country air, occasional mooing of the cows and oxen, and clucking of the chickens was a blessing I hadn't appreciated so much before. *Thank you, Lord.*

Miranda came over and began talking a mile a minute telling all she had done when we were away. Nancy and I couldn't help just laughing at how great it was to be home with family. Sarah, Mariah and Abigail put together a delicious tea with the help of Olive, and it was so good to be home in our family of girls.

Chapter 22

A Letter from Cyrus

Cyrus had not come back on Friday, so that meant we would have to wait for Monday when the stage would come again from Worcester. On Monday, we expected him to return, and Mr. Nolen went to meet the stagecoach in Northbridge Center. Instead, there were two letters—one to Mr. Nolen and one to me. Mr. Nolen had read his already and looked solemn when he came to our house and gave me mine. He just said, "Here's a letter from Cyrus," rubbed his nose and chin a bit, cleared his throat nervously and walked away.

I walked out to the apple orchard to read my letter alone. I picked a shiny red, tart, juicy apple and took one bite and began to read to myself in an Irish accent:

"My Dear Lovely Lass, Betsey,

"When I left to go visit me friend, I did not know that it would mean so much to me to be with Irish again. I began to realize how hard I had been trying to be accepted in Northbridge and Sutton by the English, well Americans really. In Worcester, there are many Irish, and 'tis wonderful to feel accepted again, to be surrounded by the Irish accents, to hear the Irish music, and there is even an Irish priest here. I didn't know how thoroughly Irish I was. I have decided to stay here and have already found a job.

"I thank your family for accepting me and even considering selling your land. I know you will make a wonderful wife for some happy lad, and I was happy thinking it would be me. Now I realize for both of our happiness, I will look for an Irish lass. Thank you for the many long walks we took and the good times we shared. I hope you will not be too mad at me for making this choice.

"I would like to visit your family again sometime, but not for a few months, I think. Thanks to Jonathan for getting me the job at the Whitin mill and for hiring me to work on your land. I can never forget your family's kindness. Give my love to each family member individually. I wrote Mr. Nolen about me new job and the land I will be able to buy here in the Irish section of Worcester.

"You'll be in me thoughts and prayers for a long time.

Sincerely,
Cyrus Delaney"

I was so stunned at first and felt upset by the shock of it, and I sat with the letter open in my lap for a few minutes and then began to cry. Sarah saw me and started to come my way, but I waved her away. I needed to think this through myself. I got up and walked deep into the apple orchard and followed the brook to Burt's pond. I prayed but don't know what I said or even if I used words and then realized that I was actually listening for God as Deacon Whipple had suggested. I didn't hear any words, but I found myself at peace and I knew God loved me and what had happened was right.

I walked back to the house saying the Lord's prayer. As I walked, I began thinking again of the phrase, "Thy will be done on earth as it is in heaven." I went in the house and found that Jonathan had hung Abigail's calligraphy on the wall. I read it softly aloud to myself. "For I am persuaded that neither death, nor life, nor angels, nor principalities, nor powers, nor things present, nor things to come, nor height, nor depth, nor any other creature, shall separate us from the love of God, which is in Christ Jesus our Lord."

I felt that I had entered a place of worship. Not that the house was a place of worship, but that between God and me there was a place of worship. I prayed silently for Cyrus, and I prayed for me. And I knew that things would never be the same again. And, with tears streaming down my face, I was content. Content to be just plain Betsey.

Postscript from the Author

Never the Same Again is based on the Samuel Carpenter family which lived in South Sutton, Massachusetts, just over the border from Northbridge, in the 1820's and 30's. The names and ages of the family members are accurate. Much of what is described really did happen, and is documented by town records, court records, deeds, etc., but I had to imagine how or why. For instance, Samuel and two-year-old Silence did die in October and November of 1826, but I do not know the cause of death. There was a baby named Harriet who was born several months following his death. Samuel Carpenter was a maker of wooden ploughs, with a workplace attached to his house. Tyley Burt Carpenter, the mother, died two years later, and several months later, there was a document signed by all the children above fourteen years of age stating that they would contribute any income to the father's estate. I used the actual wording from that document. A neighbor, George Nolen, who was 28-years old, the husband of Olive Crossman and the father of little Horace, was appointed as guardian.

The names of ministers and neighbors are accurate. Rev. Crane, a short, tobacco-chewing minister at Northbridge Congregational Church, was there for nearly fifty years, and educated hundreds of young men in his house. He owned a lot of farm land which he actively farmed himself, had the only cider mill in town, was opposed to the Temperance Movement, and was paid fifty cents to observe each of the district schools.

I do not know if Nancy ever taught school, but Rebecca Bradford really was a teacher who was responsible for getting the Methodist church started in town, because she invited her minister from Providence, Rev. Osgood, to come up and preach at Rufus Bennett's house.

I know that William moved west somewhere, probably Illinois, but I do not know where or when. I do not know if he worked on the canal or if he shot a muskrat.

I do not know if Jonathan worked at the cotton mill. I do know there was a cotton mill at that time, owned by Paul Whitin and sons. Later the mill turned to the manufacture of textile machinery and became the largest mill of that type in the world. This was largely due to the genius of John C. Whitin, who worked in the mill off and on since he was nine and who was Jonathan's age. A few years after Paul Whitin's death, a large section of Northbridge was renamed Whitinsville, and that is where I have lived for twenty-one years.

According to town records, Betsey Carpenter and a Cyrus Delaney filed an intention to marry but, in fact, never did. I do not know why, but since the last name was Irish, and there were Irish workers around from the canal work, I imagined what might have happened. During that time period, there was a considerable amount of prejudice against Irish and Catholics. A Cyrus Delaney appears in the 1850 census records of Worcester, Massachusetts, married with children. For that reason, in my book, I had him move to Worcester. Worcester at that time was noted, among other things, for its manufacturing of wire.

The grist mill no longer exists on the Carpenter property, but Burt's pond and the brook still do. They are just off Purgatory Road on Burdon Street near New Village in Whitinsville. The little brick schoolhouse is still down the road, though now it is a residence. The Second Baptist Church of South Sutton is still there, on Barnett Road, but is also now a residence. The little Lackey cemetery where the family is buried is still there, but the meadow below it is now a man-made pond, Meadow Pond, and is the main water supply for the town of Whitinsville. The Paul Whitin and Sons cotton mill original building is still there in the center of town beside the Mumford River, and is presently used for employment of mentally-challenged adults.

The Blackstone River and Canal are now a part of The Blackstone River Valley National Heritage Corridor, stretching 45 miles from Worcester, Massachusetts, to Providence, Rhode Island. A beautiful 4-mile section of canal with tow path has been partially restored and makes a lovely self-directed walk through all seasons of the year. Goat Hill lock is one of the best preserved locks on the canal and is seen on this walk; it is not functional. You may want to visit the State Park visitor's center at River Bend Farm on E. Hartford Avenue in Uxbridge to see the canal as Betsey's family would have, and go for the walk. You can still often spot one of the beautiful blue heron along the river and canal, or possibly a pheasant or a muskrat.

I hope I have helped this part of our national history come to life for you through the eyes of Betsey.

Phyllis Hosken Masso

Glossary

Auctioning the poor — There was no welfare system during this time period, but each town was responsible to take care of its poor. They did this by auctioning the poor to the lowest bidder. The family who won the bid would be paid by the town to care for the poor. For instance, the town might pay about twelve cents per week to care for a poor person. The price varied according to the poor person's age and health. The town wouldn't pay the family as much to take care of a healthy teenager who could work around the farm. They would need to pay more to have someone take care of an old, sickly person.

Ardent spirits — A term used for alcoholic beverages.

Baptists — Many Christian denominations sprinkle or pour water to baptize people into the Christian faith. Baptists immerse new converts in water to symbolize being dead to sin and resurrected to a new life in Christ.

Child tender — a small wooden playpen just big enough for a baby to sit or stand in.

Clout — a diaper which was pinned on with straight pins; safety pins weren't invented yet. Sometimes, these were not washed but just hung up to dry.

Consumption — a breathing disease, probably what we call tuberculosis.

Flash in the pan — only the tiny amount of gunpowder which was meant to ignite the pouch of gunpowder would catch fire. It would burn quickly (flash) in the little pan on the side of the gun.

Garret — An attic area which was often used as a bedroom. Often dried herbs were kept there as well.

Garter — a narrow band of knitted cloth used to tie around stockings to keep them up.

"In Defense of Fort McHenry" — was the original name of "The Star Spangled Banner," written by Francis Scott Key during the War of 1812.

Independence Day is celebrated on the Fourth of July. It was one of the biggest holidays of the year, second only to Thanksgiving, since most people did not celebrate Christmas during the 1820's.

Milking onto the ground. The cows had to be milked every day, even if there wasn't time to make cheese that day. The milk was just wasted onto the ground.

New Years — Money was seldom used between neighbors. Each one kept track of favors done and favors repaid. At New Years, they would make up the difference with cash. When someone died, however, accounts were settled shortly after the time of the death instead of waiting for New Years.

Necessary — the outhouse which was sometimes attached to the house and sometimes in the back yard. There were no flush toilets or running water.

Pews — People owned the benches, or pews, at the meeting house which is where church services were held. The ones upstairs (in the gallery) were not as desirable.

Papists — Protestant Christians referred to Roman Catholics as papists because of their belief in the authority of the pope.

Prinking was the word used for primping.

Rounders was a game similar to baseball.

Switchel was a refreshing drink made of water, molasses, and vinegar.

Temperance Movement was started to encourage people not to get drunk; however it soon began to oppose all use of alcoholic beverages.

Whey is the thin watery liquid which is left after the creamy part of the milk begins to solidify into cheese.

&c is the way "etc." (et cetera) was written.

Passing Through a Canal Lock

The locks along the Blackstone Canal helped boats ascend and descend the elevation changes between Worcester and Providence.

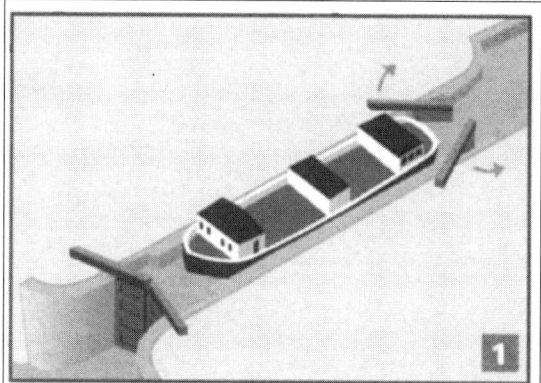

1.) The lock gates on the right are opened as the boat enters the lock and the gates on the left are closed, to let more water in, so that the boat can move down to a lower level.

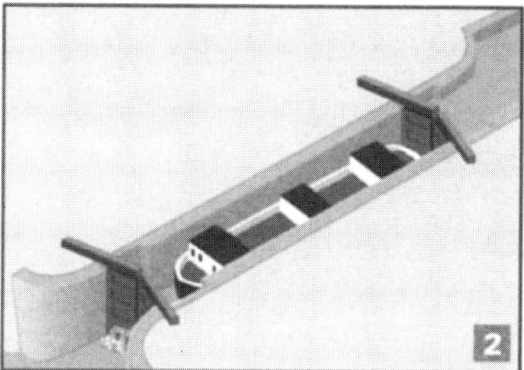

2.) Both gates are now closed.

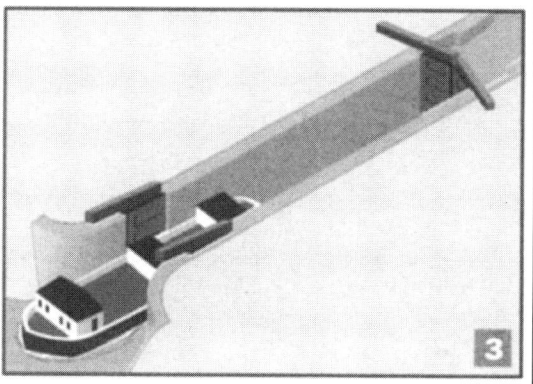

3.) The sluice gate on the left is opened, allowing water to flow out of the lock, bringing the boat to a lower level to proceed on its journey.

Courtesy of the Blackstone River Valley National Heritage Corridor.

About the Author

   Phyllis Hosken Masso grew up in Aurora, a suburb of Denver, Colorado, the fifth of six children. She graduated from Colorado State University in Fort Collins where she met her husband, Jon. They have been married thirty-two years and have lived the last twenty-eight years in New England. Twenty-two years were in the small town of Whitinsville, Massachusetts, on Carpenter Road, very near the setting of *Never the Same Again...* For nineteen years, she has been the librarian at Whitinsville Christian School.
   While living in Whitinsville, she became interested in local history, especially when the Blackstone River and Canal became a National Park Corridor. She wanted to create a book that would capture the flavor—social, economic and religious of that day.
   The author projected parts of her own life into the characters of the Carpenter family. Her own father died when she was twenty, Betsey's age, and she vividly remembers the pounding headaches and walking away from the cemetery when

she saw them shoveling the dirt on her father's coffin. She, like Sarah, is often a daydreamer; like Miranda enjoyed teaching her younger sister; like Nancy is sometimes a little preachy; and like William wanted to run away from home (and even did a couple of times for short distances). She likes to notice birds and flowers and brooks and frozen things and so she enjoyed having the opportunity to mention them in the book.

Phyllis has always liked to meet people from other countries and has, since childhood wanted to be a missionary. When her four children were high school aged and younger, she and her husband had foreign exchange students live with them from Peru, France, Italy, Japan, and Spain. She and her husband have traveled together to Guatemala, Mexico, Peru, Wales, Europe, Uganda, and Kenya sometimes for pleasure and sometimes doing short mission trips. All of her children have lived in foreign countries for a time. Living in another culture is a very broadening experience and helps you understand yourself and others better. It also makes you a more compassionate person.

Phyllis and her husband will soon be moving to Kenya to join the faculty of Daystar University, a Christian liberal arts college, where she will be working in the library and he in the science department, finally fulfilling that childhood dream of being a missionary.

Acknowledgments

Thank you to the students in the Whitinsville Christian School 5th grade history classes and their teacher, Beth Banning, who were particularly encouraging and full of ideas as I read different versions of my manuscript to them.

Old Sturbridge Village, that great living museum of the 1830's, located in Sturbridge, Massachusetts, was a constant inspiration. Interpreters were very patient with my questions as I watched cheese being made, rye being harvested, oxen being trained, fairs, entertainment, town meetings, school, Independence Day celebrations, mock funerals, weddings, and military skirmishes. The library and book store provided a wealth of information as well as the special seminars and classes on teaching of local history. Thanks to Jack Larkin and Bruce Craven for last minute checking of facts.

The park rangers at the Blackstone River Valley National Heritage Corridor also provided many answers to my questions. Special thanks to Jack Whitaker and Val Stegemoen for checking my facts and giving ideas and feedback.

The American Antiquarian Society, the Whitinsville Social Library's history room, and the Worcester Public Library were wonderful sources of information. Thanks to Atty. Henry Lane for his old maps of Sutton and Northbridge and for introducing me to probate records and deeds at the Worcester County Courthouse. A WCS middle school teacher and friend, Judy Miller, helped me do genealogical research on the Carpenter family at the New England Historic Genealogical Society in Boston, noticing details that I would have missed.

Thanks to my friend from college days, Barbara Valdois, who read early and late drafts of the manuscript carefully, giving constructive criticism and encouragement.

A medal of honor to my husband Jon, who believed I was doing something worthwhile with my time and encouraged me to keep going even if it meant simple eating, lots of visits to Old Sturbridge Village, and crazy schedules.

And just as I can see the same rivers, the school, the church, cemetery, the stone walls and some of the houses that Betsey and her family saw in their life, I feel that we share a common faith in God.